MUSTANG
Performance
and
Handling
GUIDE 1964-1985

Peter C. Sessler

Motorbooks International
Publishers & Wholesalers Inc
Osceola, Wisconsin 54020, USA ®

First published in 1985 by Motorbooks International
Publishers & Wholesalers Inc, PO Box 2, 729 Prospect Avenue, Osceola, WI 54020 USA

Motorbooks International is a certified trademark, registered with the United States Patent Office

Printed and bound in the United States of America

The information in this book is true and complete to the best of our knowledge. All recommendations are made without any guarantee on the part of the author or publisher, who also disclaim any liability incurred in connection with the use of this data or specific details

Library of Congress Cataloging in Publication Data

Sessler, Peter C.
  Mustang performance and handling guide, 1964-1985.

  1. Automobiles—Motors—Modification. 2. Automobiles—Springs and suspension—Modification. 3. Mustang automobile. I. Title.
TL210.S42 1985   629.2'5   85-2914
ISBN 0-87938-197-3 (pbk.)

Front cover photograph is a 1970 Boss 302 shot by Jerry Heasley at the Dearborn Test Track

Motorbooks International books are also available at discounts in bulk quantity for industrial or sales-promotional use. For details write to Special Sales Manager at the Publisher's address

I would like to dedicate this book to all of you who live and breathe Mustangs and especially those of you who have helped me by generously contributing your time, information, help and moral support. And a special thanks goes to my wife, Nilda, who generously contributed her time and abilities in making this book possible.

Peter C. Sessler

All photos by the author except where indicated.

CONTENTS

INTRODUCTION

Not long ago modifying your Mustang seemed to be on its way out, what with the oil crisis, and the attitude that cars were not supposed to be fun anymore but to be considered mere contrivances for transportation. Desire for any kind of performance was frowned upon in the seventies. The performance that came out of Detroit was reduced to graphics, wild paint jobs and maybe some wider than stock tires. But underneath it all what you got was a two-barrel carburetor and single exhaust. Fortunately, this trend seems to be reversing now and it's ok to have fun with your Mustang again and, behold, even Ford Motor Company shows its agreement by offering things such as TRX suspensions, four-barrel carburetors, turbocharging and the exotic SVO Mustang.

This book will attempt to show you how to get the most out of your Mustang for the least amount of money and without sacrificing comfort and streetability. Following the suggestions given will make it possible for your Mustang engine—whatever its size—to put out close to an honest one horsepower per cubic inch, which is the practical limit on the street.

True, some of the stock older big-blocks of the sixties era are pretty close to that optimum, but from 1971 on, Ford engines have suffered dramatic power cuts.

It will also be shown how to make your Mustang handle better, so much better that the people who believe that you can only get good handling from a German or Japanese car will be more than surprised.

Sometimes it must seem that most Mustang owners are involved with their cars, in every sense of the word; in fact, as some people might say, too involved. Your Mustang may just be transportation or a show car or a street performer, yet Mustang owners are a dedicated lot. It is hard to explain the satisfaction gained in working on your Mustang to someone who thinks of cars as mere appliances or status symbols. As the cliche goes, cars are extensions of ourselves and how we view ourselves. Working on your Mustang is fun and rewarding, but I have found that it can be almost a meditative experience as well. You can be completely alone, completely focused and all your everyday problems, cares, responsibilities are for a short time left behind. You have a task to complete and unlike with most things, you'll know soon if you succeeded.

The only problem that I've become aware of (and this has happened to me) is that you may get stuck with a Mustang that doesn't seem to want to be driven, only worked on. Cars do have personalities of their own. Some, no matter what you do, will always have problems cropping up, from the minor to the major. And if the car doesn't "like" you, problems always occur at the worst time and place. A good Mustang at least shows you some courtesy by deciding to break down at home when you have the replacement part in your garage. Other Mustangs, no matter how hard you drive them, will always run fine. It is my suggestion that if you have a Mustang that is giving you a hard time, sell it, no matter how much of a collectible it is. You'll never be able to fully enjoy the car because there will always be a little fear that something is going to go wrong. And because we usually attract what we fear, it will. The car may not run right for you, but it may for someone else.

This book is divided into two sections. The engine section covers the four areas of modification that I consider necessary for good performance. This is followed by explanations of how each of these areas is applied to the seven basic engine families that have been and are available on the Mustang. This section is followed by a handling chapter explaining the various modifications that are recommended and how these should be applied on the five different Mustang body groups.

Throughout this book I have stressed the point of not going overboard with any type of modification. I have seen many Mustang owners turn their Mustangs into radical street machines, creating "monsters." In order to actually drive their Mustangs more than work on them, they end up detuning them to more manageable and enjoyable levels. This book is designed so that you can avoid the costly step of making your Mustang more of a racer than a hot street machine. Of course, it is possible to make race-type components and modifications work on the street, but it requires a great deal of dedication, experimentation, time and money. I have included photos of exotic engine combinations to show what is possible. I also do not recommend turbocharging, supercharging or the use of nitrous oxide on the street. Such modifications almost always require internal engine work and you run a much greater risk of engine failure if you are not judicious with the accelerator pedal (especially with nitrous oxide).

At the same time, I have avoided going into internal engine modifications, such as balancing, boring and so on for two reasons. These are expensive modifications and their cost effectiveness on a street engine is very low. The extra few percent in horsepower that is gained is far more beneficial on a race engine. It is easy to get caught up in the numbers game.

Mustangs are fun, sporty cars. Your enjoyment will be greatly enhanced after your Mustang is modified to deliver its true potential.

Naturally, I cannot assume any liability for improper workmanship regarding any of the modifications mentioned. What I have presented here is based on hard-earned experience, not only my own, but of other enthusiasts over the last fifteen years. All information has been presented to the best of my ability and following my recommendations will definitely result in a measurable, tangible improvement in your Mustang's performance.

CHAPTER 1

THE IGNITION SYSTEM

An ignition system that functions flawlessly is of absolute importance in any engine. Spending money on other parts of the engine will be to no avail if proper combustion cannot be achieved. It's easy to go overboard here, considering the variety of ignition equipment currently available; however, this is not an area where you can afford to cut costs or skimp, either. So long as the stock system is functioning to your satisfaction the only justification for spending money on this area would be to achieve greater reliability at higher rpm and to reduce maintenance—both important in a modified engine. In my experience, the best way to go is to combine the best of what the factory offers with certain carefully picked aftermarket pieces.

From 1964-74, Mustangs used a conventional breaker-point distributor utilizing a single set of breaker points and vacuum advance. There are exceptions, such as the 271 hp 289 which used a dual-point distributor without vacuum advance. From 1975 on, Ford engines relied on an electronic ignition system, where the function of the points was electronically controlled.

The points in a conventional distributor act like a switch. They switch the battery's twelve volts on and off to the coil. Actually, it's less than twelve volts, depending on the engine, as point ignitions usually have a ballast resistor. On Ford engines, this resistance is built into the wiring to the primary (positive) side of the coil. The coil then transforms this voltage to 10,000 or more and the distributor, via the ignition wires, directs this energy to the spark plugs, according to the engine's firing order. The high-voltage energy jumps the gap between the spark plug electrodes, creating a spark, which ignites the fuel mixture. It has been estimated that in a typical engine a perfectly functioning ignition system needs about 12,000 volts to fire the spark plugs.

Electronic ignition acts exactly the same, but the switching of the current going to the coil is controlled by an electronic control box and the points are replaced by a sensor or pickup. Ford went electronic partly due to stricter emission requirements. One of the main faults of a conventional system is that points wear out and need frequent adjustment and replacement to provide peak performance. In order to maintain the mandated emission levels, a system requiring less adjustment and replacement is necessary. Electronic ignition provides peak performance all the time and seldom, if ever, needs adjustment. The only time it needs replacement is when it fails. Other advantages include higher voltage availability to the plugs, and the spark plug electrode gap may be increased, thus making a bigger spark. This is necessary in a leaned-out emission engine where combustion is more difficult to achieve.

The first modification, and a wise one, is to replace the stock Ford coil. Ever wonder why Ford coils are shorter than others? Because they are smaller and have less internal windings, they may not be able to provide the voltage needed in a modified, high-performance engine. A high-performance

A good performance coil is the first step toward a reliable ignition system. This is Autotronic's MSD Blaster 2 coil. Photo courtesy Autotronic Controls Corporation.

This coil is designed to be used with 1975- and later Ford electronic ignitions. Photo courtesy Autotronic Controls Corporation.

coil has a larger electrical reserve, which is often needed as spark plug electrodes wear and gaps increase. As plugs wear, more and more voltage is needed until finally, at high rpm, there may not be enough reserve in the stock coil to fire the plugs. A modified engine with a performance camshaft and large carburetor will have a tendency to foul the plugs at slow engine speeds, putting further strain on the stock coil. There are many aftermarket coils to choose from and they are one of the cheapest ways to achieve greater spark energy.

Another point worth mentioning is the placement of coils. Most Ford coils are mounted on the engine. Engine vibration is the number one cause of coil failure, as the vibration eventually breaks down the coil's internal windings. This is especially true in engines having a hot camshaft, which causes greater engine vibration. It is a good idea, in this case, to mount the coil on the inner fender where vibration won't be a problem. Most four-cylinder engines have their coils mounted on the inner fender because of their inherent vibration characteristics.

Many Mustang owners have converted their conventional ignition systems to electronic ones. The reasons are reduced maintenance, much greater spark energy and greater reliability. There are many systems available, and most work quite well, but there are some that can be more convenient to use.

Most electronic systems available today are either magnetic impulse (of which there are many variations), various crank trigger systems (for racing only) or the LED (light emitting diode) type. These systems use a pickup to replace the points and have a control box that must be mounted somewhere

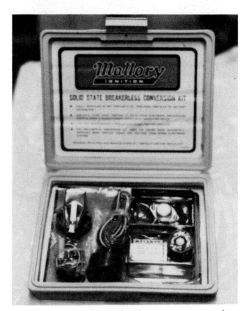

This is a typical breakerless conversion kit. Module has to be mounted in engine compartment.

Mallory's Unilite offers reliable performance in a very compact package.

in the engine compartment. The most compact of these is Mallory's Unilite system, an LED system that fits under the distributor cap. There is no control box to mount. It is easy to install since there are only three wires to connect—two to the coil and one to the ground. Stock engine appearance can thereby be maintained. The Unilite has proven to be extremely reliable in a number of engines.

Ford engines would probably best be served by a combination of electronic ignition with a multispark system, of which Autotronic Controls Corporation's MSD is the best known. During a firing cycle, rather than one spark, a series of sparks (usually up to twenty) is delivered to the spark plug and the results are obvious: much better combustion, noticeable improvement in idle quality, elimination of misfiring, the ability to fire fouled plugs and, depending on the engine, more power. According to one source, in engines with large, open combustion-chamber designs, power can be improved as much as three percent. One such design is the 351C 2V version. One other advantage of an MSD is that total advance can be reduced by 2-4 degrees and still achieve the same performance.

Autotronic makes several models that Ford engines can use. The MSD-6 provides about the most power that is required for a modified street engine, while basically stock engines can use the MSD-5. The MSD-7, which

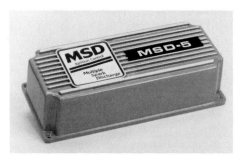

The MSD-5 and MSD-6A can be used on the street with excellent results. The MSD-7AL is strictly for competition use. Photos courtesy Autotronic Controls Corporation.

provides an incredible amount of electrical energy, is too much for the typical stock Ford distributor cap and wires.

There is one other product that Autotronic produces that is probably of interest to Mustang owners with older, high-compression engines. They call it Ping Control. By means of a dash-mounted dial, the driver can manually adjust timing from inside the car. In this way, timing can be advanced during cruising for better economy, or retarded during acceleration to reduce "ping." Retarding the timing can also be used to compensate for poor-quality gas.

It is also important that a better grade of spark plug wires be used in a performance engine, as well as other distributor components. Stock carbon-core ignition wires are prone to damage when handled in a less than delicate manner, and at best only last up to two years. Solid-core wires are preferred but they can cause radio interference on the AM band (FM reception generally won't be affected). Again, those requiring supression wires have a variety to choose from in the aftermarket.

Another area of vital importance in a performance engine is spark advance. Depending on engine timing, the spark plugs are fired a certain number of degrees before the piston reaches the top of its stroke, usually 0-12 degrees. This is to give the fuel mixture a chance to ignite (this is not instantaneous) and expand, and thus drive the piston down on its power stroke. At higher rpm, the fuel mixture still needs the same amount of time to ignite, but because the engine is turning faster, the piston would be on its way down before the fuel mixture ignited. The spark-advance mechanism in the distributor allows the spark timing to "keep up" with engine speed. This means that the spark has to be fired much earlier at higher rpm to compensate for engine speed. The centrifugal advance mechanism in the distributor advances the spark as engine speed increases and retards it as speed decreases.

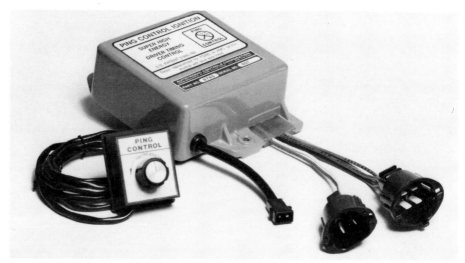

Autotronic's Ping Control allows the driver to control timing trom inside the car. Photo courtesy Autotronic Controls Corporation.

The rate of advance is controlled by two springs found underneath the distributor's breaker plate. Most factory distributors are calibrated to deliver full centrifugal advance by 4000 rpm or so. By simply changing the springs to lighter ones the engine will accelerate quicker, resulting in better throttle response and more low end power. Mr. Gasket Company makes an inexpensive kit, No. 925D, which contains two springs to fit Ford distributors. A rule of thumb is to give the engine as much advance as it can tolerate without pinging; this will require some experimentation. Probably the best thing to do is to have the distributor recalibrated professionally. However, just replacing the heavier stock spring with one from Mr. Gasket will result in a very noticeable improvement. This simple and inexpensive little modification is highly recommended for all Ford engines.

Changing the distributor springs changes the rate of advance. To change the amount of centrifugal advance, the distributor cam assembly must be changed. Stock distributors come with assemblies having two settings. By simply removing the retaining ring from the top of the distributor shaft and rotating the assembly to the other position, you change the amount of centrifugal advance. The plates are usually stamped, with two numbers; for example, 10L and 15L, meaning ten and fifteen degrees. The plate assemblies are interchangeable so that other combinations are possible to arrive at the exact requirements for your engine.

Most Ford distributors have some form of vacuum advance. This is additional spark advance controlled by the engine's vacuum. When engine vacuum is high, such as when the car is cruising, the engine can tolerate more advance than the centrifugal advance provides. This results in better mpg. It should never be disconnected as it is worth 2-3 mpg. Most Ford vacuum canisters can be adjusted to give more or less advance. In addition some Ford engines utilize a dual-advance vacuum canister. In this case, the inner orifice should be plugged and the outer one routed to a direct vacuum

Mr. Gasket's number 925D advance curve kit makes changing your distributor's advance curve a snap.

The distributor's breaker plate must be removed to expose the springs.

source on the carburetor. On most Holley carburetors, this would be on the base plate and not on the metering block.

A point worth noting about distributor recalibration is that most sixties-era distributors have more centrifugal advance and less vacuum advance. Emission distributors of the seventies tend to have less centrifugal and more vacuum advance.

It may require some experimentation to arrive at the optimum centrifugal and vacuum advance curves for your engine. (One way is to advance until you get ping, then back off.) The results are very impressive and noticeable in terms of power, acceleration and economy.

Distributor cam assemblies are interchangeable, allowing for spark advance modification.

This Shelby 302 is typical of an engine having performance ignition components: aftermarket spark plug wires, high-quality distributor cap and vacuum advance for good street operation.

It is important to remember that a properly functioning ignition system allows the engine to produce all the horsepower it was designed to make. This is the reason behind the switch by manufacturers to electronic ignitions. From their point of view, the efficiency of an electronic system, although more expensive, allows them to comply with emission certification standards. Also, from the performance point of view, this is one area where advances in technology have advanced the performance potential of pre-emission engines as well.

CHAPTER 2

THE INDUCTION SYSTEM

The search for more power leads the typical enthusiast to consider modifying an engine by installing a new aluminum intake manifold and, usually, a Holley four-barrel carburetor. There are so many manifolds to choose from and so many differences among the types available that it's very easy to make a mistake and wind up with an engine that puts out less horsepower than you started with. However, there are specific rules that can be used.

For the street, for example, use a single four-barrel system. Multiple carburetion, such as tripower and dual-quad systems, will outperform a single four-barrel system but only when a motor has been designed to use all that carburetion (that means a race engine). Many street enthusiasts do use such exotic combinations but it's quite likely they have spent many, many hours dialing in that particular combination. For the typical Mustang owner planning to use a four-barrel system, the question is which type and why.

The first step is to find out what the factory has available. During the sixties, Ford introduced a slew of performance manifolds, with extensive Ford engineering behind them. They are still very popular. The old FE Series engines (390, 427, 428) provide the largest selection to choose from—single four-barrels, dual-quads, tripower, Weber manifolds—followed by the 289/302 small-blocks. The later and more modern engine series, such as the 335 Series (351C) and the 385 Series (429), provide less variety. They were introduced late in the muscle car era, when Ford was backing away from its performance stance. These manifolds are mostly available through the many Ford parts vendors who specialize in used Ford engine parts.

Most Ford factory manifolds are of the dual-plane type known as the Cross-H or 180-degree design, originated by Ford in the early thirties. With this type, each half of the manifold feeds half the cylinders, and the two halves are not connected. It is called a 180-degree because the engine draws alternately from each manifold half as it moves through the firing cycle. The

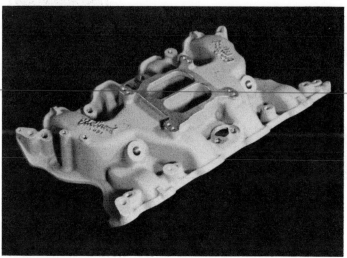

A strong street performer is the single four-barrel high-rise manifold. This one is for the 351C. Photo courtesy Edelbrock Corporation.

The name Holley has been synonymous with performance for the past 25 years. This Holley four-barrel flows 780 cfm and is stock on the Boss 302 engine. Most high-performance Holleys have manual chokes.

dual-plane manifold provides excellent throttle response and low- to mid-range power. However, it tends to become restrictive at high rpm.

The typical stock intake manifold is made of cast iron and is purposely made restrictive and low for hood clearance. The bulk of Ford engines came with (and still do) a small two-barrel carburetor. Typical Ford performance intakes, such as those in the Boss 302 or the Shelby Mustang 306 hp 289, are made of aluminum (for weight saving) and are known as high-rise manifolds. Basically, these are refined dual-plane manifolds that follow stock configuration but have taller, larger passages for better engine breathing. Ford, like most of its competitors, used larger than necessary carburetors on these engines. The Boss 302 came with a Holley 780 cubic feet per minute (cfm) unit and the Shelby 289 came with a 715 cfm unit. Due to the manifold's high efficiency, it maintained the necessary mixture velocity for sharp response, while the large carburetor helped to overcome the restrictive nature of the dual-plane design at high rpm.

The dual-plane high-rise is still a popular choice and you really can't go wrong with such a manifold, particularly when big-block Mustangs with automatic transmission are involved.

The other single four-barrel design that has been used successfully is the single-plane or X-type manifold. Here, all the manifold runners are connected to a common chamber or plenum and are fed by a single carburetor. It is a simple design which, generally, was not very popular on the street. In the late sixties, Edelbrock refined its design to provide superior perfor-

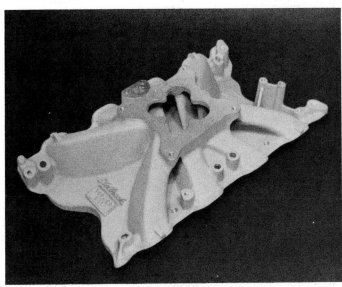

The newer X-type single-plane manifolds are much less restrictive than the dual-plane high-rise, yet give equal low end performance. This is Edelbrock's Torker 351 for the 351C. Photo courtesy Edelbrock Corporation.

mance over the dual-plane design. These manifolds have been developed and refined to such an extent that they match the low- and mid-range response of the dual-plane manifolds while surpassing them at higher rpm. Most, if not all, of the newer X-type manifolds look very much alike. Usually it will be best to follow the manufacturer's recommendations according to your intended usage.

How much better are the X-types than the dual-plane manifolds? Edelbrock made a series of tests when it introduced its Torker 289, a single-plane manifold for the 289/302 engine. (The results are reproduced here for your consideration.) Edelbrock's F-4B manifold is very similar to Ford's Cobra high-rise intake (dual-plane) and can be used as a comparison point between the two designs. The engine used was a blueprinted 302 with a Ford

Engine rpm	Stock 350 cfm two-barrel & manifold	Stock manifold & 500 cfm Holley two-barrel List #4412	Edelbrock F-4B Holley four-barrel List #4118 725 cfm
2500	126	135	122
3000	153	166	149
3500	174	189	180
4000	188	207	213
4500	204	224	233
5000	206	229	245
5500	201	228	244
6000	188	—	236

Engine rpm	Torker 289 & Holley four-barrel List #4118 725 cfm	Torker 289 & Holley two-barrel List #6425 650 cfm	Torker 289 & Autolite four-barrel 600 cfm
2500	129	113	119
3000	159	150	144
3500	188	180	175
4000	222	210	209
4500	256	240	242
5000	270	254	259
5500	267	251	258

Engine rpm	Torker 289 & Holley four-barrel List #6619 600 cfm
2500	128
3000	157
3500	187
4000	218
4500	251
5000	264
5500	274
6000	261

mechanical cam, Accel distributor, stock compression and dyno-headers. The results are interesting, to say the least.

The stock two-barrel intake seems to hold its own up to 3500 rpm; from then on, power increase slows down considerably. With the simple addition of a Holley 500 cfm two-barrel, there is a 23 hp increase at 5000 rpm, definitely a cheap and easy way to get more power for those on a budget.

The F-4B high-rise with the 725 cfm Holley peaks at 5000 rpm. It is likely that this particular manifold would do better with a smaller 600 cfm carburetor.

The Torker 289 intake, even with the 650 cfm two-barrel, outdoes the F-4B with a Holley four-barrel. The less restrictive nature of the single-plane design is evident, as the 302's power peak is reached at 5500 rpm, probably where the cam peaks. The best combination is with the Holley 600 cfm carburetor, proving that bigger is not always better.

The Torker 289 is good for at least a 30 hp increase over the dual-plane intake, and with a four-barrel, more than 70 hp over stock. This is a tremendous return on a very simple investment. Bear in mind, however, that these results were obtained with a blueprinted, modified 302. You can't put a Torker on a stock 302 and expect the same results, although the same percentage increase of power is likely.

Picking a performance carburetor can be a headache due to the great selection to choose from in many different cfm ratings.

There is a tendency with many individuals new to the modification of engines to choose a carburetor that is too large for a particular application. This usually results in poor performance and low mpg. The recommendations made in each engine chapter are based upon experience and are intended to provide good performance with the least amount of maintenance and retuning. If you want reliable and strong street performance, follow the recommendations carefully.

This is a Rochester Quadrajet four-barrel which exemplifies the spreadbore design. Most flow about 700 cfm. The Quadrajet was standard equipment on the 429CJ engines.

The typical Holley has primaries and secondaries that are more equal to each other. This is better for performance but hurts economy.

If you aren't knowledgeable about carburetion and fine tuning, stay with a vacuum secondary carburetor. All Ford Holley carburetors are vacuum secondary units. Although Holley's Double Pumpers are sometimes difficult to calibrate on automatic, high-geared (low numerical axle ratio) Mustangs, they can be made to work and they do provide superior performance. Holley offers two Double Pumpers with throttle linkage that accepts Ford's automatic transmission kickdown rod. List number 6708 is rated at 650 cfm, and list number 6709 is rated at 750 cfm.

You can combine good mileage with performance if you use one of Holley's spreadbore-design carburetors, which features very small primaries and large secondaries. These are designed to fit spreadbore manifolds. Most Ford manifolds will require an adapter. These carburetors are available in either Double-Pumper or vacuum secondary form.

Those of you on a budget can retain the stock two-barrel manifold on a

A rare ram-box intake for the 289/302. It is designed for high rpm use—a single four-barrel X-type manifold will outperform it on the street.

Used Holley carburetors are plentiful at shows and swap meets, particularly Ford-application Holleys.

Successful factory ram air systems include the 1969-70 428CJ Shaker and the 1971-73 Mustang ram air. The Shaker is good for 0.2 second in the quarter mile.

V-8 engine and use Holley's list number 4412 two-barrel rated at 500 cfm. This is an excellent carburetor which will give you an honest 20-25 hp on a 289/302 and more on a 351, and has the automatic kickdown linkage.

Of course there are other brands to choose from (such as Carter), but the overwhelming majority rely on Holley because they are reliable and extremely easy to modify, adjust and fine tune. (I suggest reading any of the Holley books listed in the back of this book for more information.)

Another point worth considering involves air cleaners. Here, the rule is "the bigger the better." A small air cleaner will rob horsepower from your engine because it won't allow enough air to flow through the carburetor. It's a lot like having a long-distance runner run with a handkerchief in his mouth.

For example, in HP Books' *Holley Carburetors and Manifolds* there are tests showing the effects on airflow of a stock single snorkel air cleaner versus modified air cleaners. In Holley's tests, a stock single-snorkel air

An example of a bad ram air system is found on the 1969-70 Boss 429 Mustangs. The owner of this one wisely replaced the stock air cleaner with an efficient Moroso unit.

cleaner limited airflow to 480 cfm on a carburetor that flowed 713 cfm without an air cleaner. In all cases, using an aftermarket air cleaner setup dramatically improved flow to varying degrees, but if you are on a budget you can also improve your air cleaner's performance by using a taller than stock element (which in effect makes your air cleaner an open-element unit) or by the old hot-rod standby, inverting your stock air cleaner lid to let more air flow in. An exposed element will have to be changed frequently if you drive in dusty conditions.

Obviously, a stock air cleaner is almost useless from the performance

One of the simplest induction modifications is to invert the stock air cleaner lid, thereby making an open-element air cleaner.

Stock air cleaners are very restrictive.

Most engines from the seventies have the fresh-air systems. The owner of this 351C added a snorkel to maintain factory appearance. However, it is not as free-flowing as an open-element air cleaner.

point of view, as it restricts airflow by one-third. There are many performance air cleaners on the market today, and it is strongly suggested that one is used.

At this point it may be worth mentioning the current fuel situation. Some of the older Ford high-performance engines with high compression find it

Although better than a stock air cleaner, this one is still restrictive because of its small size.

Guaranteed no restrictions with this Moroso-equipped 351C. Note taller element.

With the exception of the Paxton supercharger, these exotic induction systems are impractical for the street.

very difficult to run on regular and unleaded premium gas that is currently available. If your engine has a compression ratio of greater than 10.5:1 you are probably already using some sort of additive—and this is expensive.

If you are in the position of rebuilding your engine it probably is worthwhile to reduce compression to a more tolerable 10:1 ratio. By far the most common remedy is to mix regular leaded gas with an equal amount of unleaded premium which can yield an octane of 95-96. Mixing gas along with a device such as Autotronic's Ping Control, which enables you to adjust timing from inside the car, is about the most cost effective way of dealing with the lower-octane-rating gasolines that are currently available.

It's hard to resist the allure of dual-quads or some other exotic-looking intake setup but if you are interested in impressive street performance, the least expensive and most effective induction system is still a single four-barrel carburetor on a performance intake manifold.

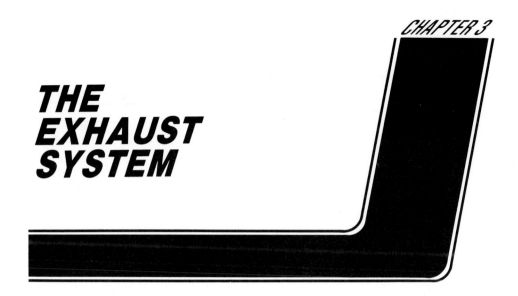

CHAPTER 3

THE EXHAUST SYSTEM

Modifying your engine's exhaust system is mandatory if you want more power. Even the factory's best performance exhaust systems leave much to be desired. The truth is, even some rather basic modifications will improve performance.

The single exhaust system, which is fine for regular everyday use, can tend to be very restrictive. The restrictions become much more obvious when the engine is modified to any extent. For instance, doubling your engine's power will increase backpressure by 400 percent. The goal of any exhaust system modifications is to reduce backpressure as much as possible so that the power the engine produces can be used. There are those who feel that some engines perform "better" with some backpressure in the exhaust system, but if you test two identical engines that have their timing and carburetion set for best performance, it becomes obvious that the engine with the less restrictive exhaust system will put out more horsepower.

The majority of Mustangs have a single exhaust system. Therefore, the simplest way to get some extra horsepower is to convert to a dual exhaust system. Assuming the pipes are available, converting to a factory dual exhaust system is obviously beneficial, but factory duals tend to be more restrictive than aftermarket or homemade dual exhaust systems. Most of the high-performance Mustangs of the later sixties came with a dual exhaust system that utilized a single transverse muffler mounted between the gas tank and rear axle. However, in 1970, Mustangs used two mufflers that fit underneath the rear seat cavities. This resulted in a more efficient exhaust system. Some Mustangs also had a dealer-installed exhaust system of this design. If you are going for duals, it is best to try to copy this system, as it is inherently more efficient than the single transverse muffler.

There are now aftermarket kits to convert any car to a dual exhaust system. Cyclone markets such a kit, which comes with two turbo-type mufflers and can hook up to stock pipes or tube headers. The system, though, exits in front of the rear wheels, much like the 1965 GT350 Shelby Mustang. For stock exit, factory tail pipes, depending on the application,

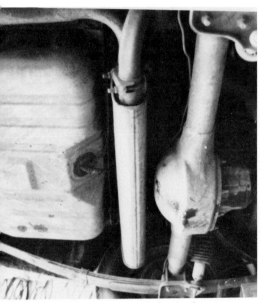

1964½-69 Mustangs used a single transverse muffler sandwiched between the axle and gas tank.

Stock, dual exhaust pipes for 1967-69 Mustangs can usually be found at swap meets. Because they are restrictive, they are only recommended if strict originality is required.

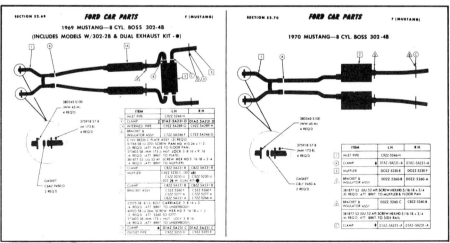

You can adapt the 1970-type dual exhaust system to your earlier Mustang for better performance.

can be used. All Ford dual exhaust systems used a cross-over pipe, which helps power and reduces overall sound level. This should be incorporated in systems that don't already have it.

Another point worth remembering is that Ford duals with the transverse mufflers suffer from restrictive pipes. For instance, on 428CJ Mustangs, the

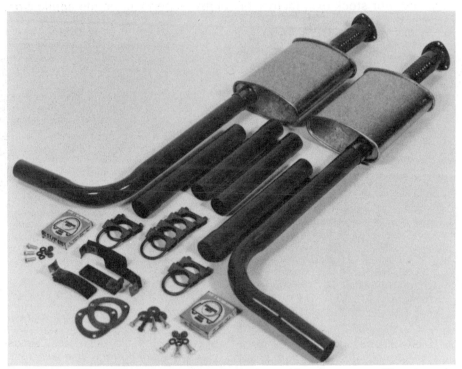

This aftermarket dual exhaust kit uses 2¼ inch pipes with turbo-type mufflers. It can be used with headers or stock exhaust manifolds. Photo courtesy American Exhaust Industries (Cyclone).

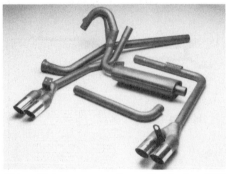

This efficient system is available for 1979 and later Mustangs. Photo courtesy DOBI.

You can also have a custom-made system on your Mustang. This is a 1979 302 Mustang that really needs exhaust improvement. Brad Davis photo.

pipes nominally measure 2¼ inches yet they neck down to under two inches where they are bent to clear the axle—obviously a major restriction.

The next item after duals to be considered is mufflers. There has been constant research and development in this area and it seems that every manufacturer is constantly improving its mufflers or incorporating some new design feature. Most of these are called "turbo" mufflers, modeled after the units first used on the Chevrolet turbocharged Corvair. Many perform as well or better than the original and many perform much worse because of reduced flow.

It is difficult to make specific recommendations regarding which turbo muffler is best. In *Performance with Economy,* by David Vizard, several of these were tested. Listed below are the top six turbo mufflers in terms of cfm rating:

1. Supreme Super C 111224 2½ inch diameter   355
2. Arvin Industries turbo 2½ inch diameter   332
3. GM turbo 2½ inch diameter (original equipment)   293
4. Midas turbo 2½ inch diameter   279
5. IPC hp 250 turbo 2½ inch diameter   279
6. Walker Red Line 2½ inch diameter   275

The only problem with these tests is that they were done back in 1981. Other manufacturers' mufflers that were also tested and didn't do as well have long since been replaced with models with better flowing units, particularly those by Thrush and Cyclone.

One point of interest is that all the mufflers tested had the large 2½ inch inlet. Regardless of the pipe you are using in your exhaust system, always use the muffler with the largest inlet and core available. For instance, a 2¼ inch inlet muffler will flow less than one with a 2½ inch inlet and core. Use the

Most mufflers look the same on the outside, but the way they are constructed internally makes a tremendous difference. Photo courtesy American Exhaust Industries.

larger muffler with an adaptor to fit your exhaust pipe. Conversely, do not reduce the size of the exhaust pipe with an adaptor to fit a smaller muffler.

Glasspack mufflers aren't recommended for several reasons. First, they are loud and attract unnecessary attention. Second, they do not last as long as conventional mufflers. If you must use a glasspack, try to match the inlet

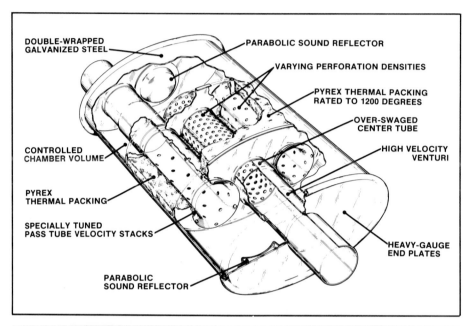

DOUBLE-WRAPPED
GALVANIZED STEEL

PARABOLIC SOUND REFLECTOR

VARYING PERFORATION DENSITIES

PYREX THERMAL PACKING
RATED TO 1200 DEGREES

OVER-SWAGED
CENTER TUBE

CONTROLLED
CHAMBER VOLUME

HIGH VELOCITY
VENTURI

PYREX
THERMAL PACKING

SPECIALLY TUNED
PASS TUBE VELOCITY STACKS

HEAVY-GAUGE
END PLATES

PARABOLIC
SOUND REFLECTOR

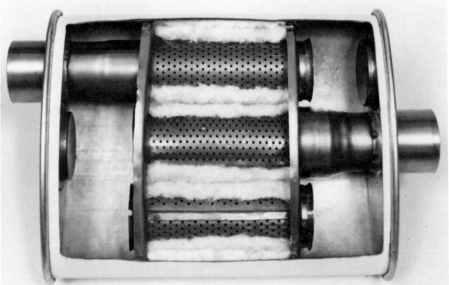

This is a cutaway of Cyclone's Sonic Turbo muffler. The parabolic sound reflectors at each end deflect the sound to the Pyrex thermal packing for absorption. Photo courtesy American Exhaust Industries.

pipe and core size with the exhaust pipe you are using. Also, look through the muffler before you buy it. If you see the internal louvers protruding, it is likely that this particular muffler will not allow as much flow as one with louvers punched outward. Because glasspacks are loud, it may be necessary to use two mufflers per side. Be prepared to change back to conventional mufflers, because after a week or two, their allure may quickly fade.

The next item to consider, and this is applicable to the Mustang II and newer Mustangs, is the use of catalytic converters. These devices resemble mufflers and work in conjunction with the rest of the engine's emission

This is a cutaway of Thrush's old Turbo 500, now discontinued. Note restrictive inlet and outlet tubes. Photo courtesy Thrush Incorporated.

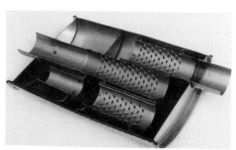

Thrush's new Turbo 500 Series number 570 features larger passage tubes. Photo courtesy Thrush Incorporated.

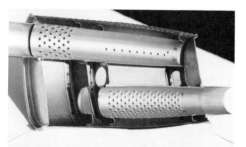

This is a cutaway of a Hush Thrush number 527. Photo courtesy Thrush Incorporated.

Here is Thrush's Turbo 400 Series number 490. Photo courtesy Thrush Incorporated.

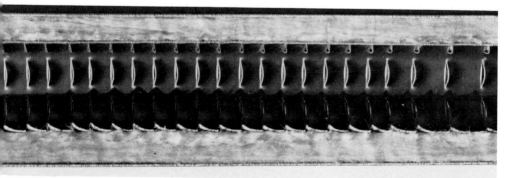

This is a typical glasspack muffler. The fiberglass absorbs sound through the slats cut in the center pipe. However, a good turbo muffler is not only quieter, but less restrictive. Photo courtesy Thrush Incorporated.

system to remove pollutants from the exhaust. Ford types, which use a honeycomb design, are less restrictive than other converters; nevertheless, they are restrictive. As you may know, it is illegal to remove the converter in some states, but if you use your Mustang off-road, you can substitute one of the many available "test pipes," which eliminate the converter for better engine performance and higher mpg. In fact, many enthusiasts seem to be conducting long-term "tests" by leaving these pipes on permanently.

There are certain facts that should be considered concerning catalytic converters, in addition to the fact that they are restrictive. Leaded fuel, for example, will contaminate the catalytic agent and render it inoperable. Running an excessively rich mixture will do the same. For instance, if your carburetor's choke sticks and your engine produces lots of black smoke, your catalytic converter will no longer function. A misfiring engine, due to a bad spark plug or defective spark plug wire, will also ruin a converter. Hard starting with lots of pumping of the gas pedal to get the engine going will ruin it as well, because this also results in a rich mixture. Considering these relatively common problems, it becomes obvious that there are millions of cars on the road with useless catalytic converters.

The last important item to consider is exhaust headers. Any well-designed header is better than the stock exhaust manifolds. The stock manifolds, while durable, compact and cheap to produce, are efficient only at very low engine speeds. As rpm increases to middle and upper ranges, they become very restrictive because they cause turbulence and pressure pulses which obstruct exhaust flow. Headers tend to make more power in relation to the engine's modifications. A modified engine will have a greater power increase with headers than a stock engine with headers. However, a

Headers provide a substantial boost in power. These are for a 1979 and later 302 Mustang. Photo courtesy DOBI.

Header installation is tough on big-block Mustangs. Note lack of clearance on this 428CJ.

351C should produce an additional 25-50 hp with just the addition of headers. This is a substantial gain. Remember, though, that it is always necessary to recalibrate the carburetor and adjust engine timing when headers are installed; otherwise you will experience a power loss.

There are some general rules that can apply to headers and engines. For high-rpm power, the header should have short yet large-diameter pipes and a large-diameter collector. For low-rpm efficiency, the pipes should be smaller and longer with a small-diameter collector.

Generally speaking, engines in the 302-351 range should have headers in the 1¾-inch-diameter range with pipes measuring 30-36 inches long. Smaller-diameter pipes will give better economy at the expense of some upper-rpm horsepower gain. A good header for the popular 302 would measure 1⅝ inches.

Big-blocks can use headers measuring 1¾-2 inches in diameter. Several manufacturers make 2⅛ and 2¼ inch headers for these engines, but for better street performance it is best to stay with smaller-diameter pipes. Most header manufacturers follow these general guidelines.

In the past few years, the antireversion header has become popular because it combines the economy of small-diameter pipe headers with the greater horsepower potential of a large-diameter pipe header. This is done with antireversion cones at the flange, which allows normal exhaust flow, yet discourages reverse flow. Reverse flow occurs in most engines, especially during low-rpm operation, and this reduces mileage. Because this header design helps mileage, your carburetor's jets will have to be reduced two to four sizes when switching from a conventional header.

Certainly there are advantages to headers, but they may be difficult to install in big-block-equipped Mustangs. 428CJ-equipped Mustangs have

There is no header clearance problem on small-blocks.

very tight engine compartments and they are very fast already. You can get substantial horsepower gains from just changing to a freer-flowing exhaust system but, of course, if you are prepared for the effort required, headers are very beneficial. For Mustangs with smaller engines and roomier engine compartments, headers are highly recommended.

A carefully thought out and constructed exhaust system will let your engine make the power it was designed to put out. Considering the cost and relative ease of installation, it is hard to overlook this area.

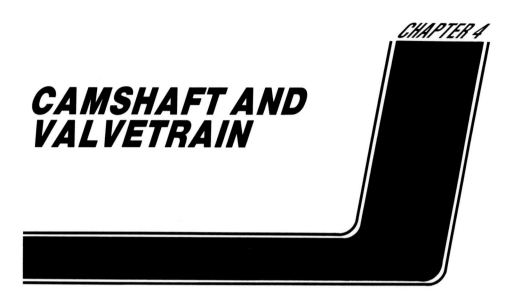

CHAPTER 4

CAMSHAFT AND VALVETRAIN

So far the modifications touched upon have left us with a much more efficient and powerful, yet relatively stock, engine. The modifications are designed to bring out the maximum the engine can produce in its essentially stock configuration. Changing the camshaft will alter performance and affect the intake, exhaust system, relative economy and driveability of your Mustang. It is not something to be taken lightly and a mistake made in choosing the cam will not only result in a poorly running street Mustang, but will also create additional work to get the car back into proper street condition.

The typical stock cam found in most Ford engines was designed for smoothness and low end power to provide long, trouble-free performance. Changing to a performance cam will move the power-producing characteristics up the rpm range of the engine. The problem with selecting a cam is to figure out how far to move up the power curve without hurting low end performance and mileage. The goal should be to choose a cam that will increase power over stock without losing the economy of a stock cam. How much power should a cam change provide? A good target is an increase of about ten percent.

There are two areas in cam design that affect the engine's power curve: lift and duration. A cam with more valve lift will generally produce more power than a cam with less lift. However, there are practical mechanical limits to increasing the amount of lift. For street use it is around 0.500 inch. The big advantage of increased lift is that it produces more power, yet driveability and fuel economy remain the same.

Duration is the amount of time, measured in degrees, that the valves are left open to allow the fuel mixture to enter and leave the combustion chamber. Obviously the longer the duration, the greater mixture and the more power the engine will produce. The problem with long duration is that it will reduce low end performance and economy. It is essential, therefore, to find a cam that combines reasonably high lift with duration short enough to allow good low end performance.

Most aftermarket cam manufacturers have a wide selection of cams that can provide more lift with duration figures similar to stock Ford cams. They also usually have hotter cams that increase in duration in small incremental steps. For instance, Crane Cams has its Blazer and Fireball series cams which are designed for good street performance; Competition Cams has its High Energy Cam series, consisting of seven different basic grinds, each a little stronger than the previous, from an RV-type grind to a "pro street" wild-type grind. Each manufacturer lists in its catalog what is best for your particular car according to the modifications already made on your engine. Remember that the hotter the cam, the greater the necessity of complementing that cam with the rest of the engine—meaning larger carburetor, exhaust headers, stronger valve springs and so on.

One of the difficulties in choosing a cam has to do with duration and, specifically, how it is measured. Most aftermarket cam companies measure duration at 0.050 inch valve lift. Ford does not, so it can be difficult compar-

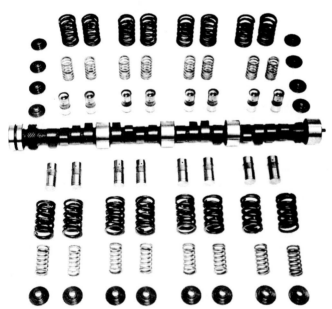

Typical camshaft kit includes a new cam, lifters, springs and retainers. It is also recommended that you change valve seals and valve locks. Photo courtesy Maier Racing Enterprises.

ing stock Ford cam duration with those offered by aftermarket manufacturers. Listed here are some popular stock Ford cams with Ford duration figures and comparable durations measured at 0.050 inch lift, which should be very helpful.

ENGINE	STOCK HP	FORD DURATION		DURATION AT 0.050 INCH	
		Intake	Exhaust	Intake	Exhaust
289	200, 225	266	244	182	180
289HP*	271, 306	310	310	232	232
351CJ	266	270	290	190	202
390GT	320, 325	270	290	224	232
428CJ	335	270	290	224	232
429SCJ*	370, 375	300	300	232	232
*solid lifters					

The stock 289HP, 390GT, 428CJ and 429CJ cams are pretty healthy from a performance point of view, although for better street performance a little more lift wouldn't hurt. But regarding duration, they are close to the maximum that is considered streetable. See chart.

DURATION AT 0.050 INCH CAM LIFT	RPM RANGE
200	1000-4000
210	1300-4500
220	1500-5500
230	2300-6000
240	3000-7000
250	3800-7500
260	4200-8000

A practical limit for street operation is cams with 230-240 degree duration. This type of cam will have the uneven idle associated with performance cams with a power curve beginning around 2500 rpm and trailing off between 6000 and 6800 rpm.

There is really no point in choosing a mechanical lifter camshaft over a hydraulic cam. A hydraulic cam is maintenance free and easier on the valvetrain, and there are no sacrifices in power or economy. Depending on the engine, anti-pump-up hydraulic lifters can provide top rpm of 7000 or so, more than enough for the street.

When thinking of hydraulic lifters, it is worth considering the Rhoads variable rate lifters. These lifters are basically modified stock hydraulic lifters, designed to bleed off oil below 3500 rpm. This reduces cam lift and duration. As engine rpm increases, the oil is retained in the lifter restoring full cam duration and lift. This can be especially important for an engine with a cam that may be too wild for good low end operation. By reducing lift and duration at low rpm, low end driveability and economy is restored. Looking at it from another angle, you can install a much more radical hydraulic cam in your engine and still retain good low end response. They really work. For example, my 1969 Boss 429 with a Reed cam (0.570/0.596 lift and 240/244 duration) was awful in traffic, and the slightest incline required downshifting to first gear at speeds below 35 mph. With the Rhoads lifters, low end response was amazingly improved. The 429's idle speed was also reduced to a bearable 900 rpm, and fuel economy went from 7 mpg to 11 mpg with dual-quads.

Specific recommendations are made in each engine chapter, but there are still certain facts that pertain to all engines. Changing a cam will almost always require taking off the cylinder heads and modifying them for larger springs, screw-in studs and any other valve work that may be needed. Always replace the stock timing gear and chain with a stronger double-roller setup and follow to the letter the manufacturer's installation and break-in instructions. Changing a cam is expensive and should only be attempted after modifications in the intake and exhaust system are completed.

Another point to consider is that installing a cam with high rpm potential means that the rest of the valvetrain must also be upgraded. This in turn means new pushrods, retainers and rocker arms, which add to the cost. With

A performance timing gear and chain is a must, such as this roller type. Photo courtesy Maier Racing Enterprises.

This is typical of a fully prepped small-block cylinder head, with rocker arm studs and guide plates. Photo courtesy Maier Racing Enterprises.

many Ford engines, higher rpm also means oiling system modifications. Picking a milder performance cam enables you to stay with stock components thus lowering cost.

Problems that are associated with a cam that is too radical for a street car are: poor idle and fuel economy, high idle speed, hard starting, fouling of spark plugs, overheating, loading-up in traffic and accelerated valve-guide wear. It is better to be conservative and not go overboard.

Aluminum roller rocker arms aren't necessary for the street; however, they do add a measure of reliability to your valvetrain if you can afford them.

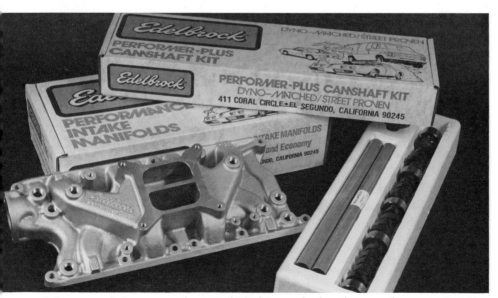

It is extremely important that camshafts be matched to the rest of your engine. Here Edelbrock has combined a performance dual-plane manifold with a matched camshaft. Photo courtesy Edelbrock Corporation.

CHAPTER 5

ADDITIONAL MODIFICATIONS AND TIPS

Modifying your engine for more power will put additional strain on your Mustang's driveline. With most Mustangs, especially the 1964-73 models, there is plenty of built-in reserve but this is less so on the newer 1974 and later Mustangs. Even so, once you've modified your engine it is a good idea to look at the rest of your Mustang, even if you happen to own one of the rarer performance Mustangs such as the Boss or Shelby, which are already equipped with heavy-duty components.

AUTOMATIC TRANSMISSIONS

The majority of Mustangs have automatic transmissions. The well-known C-6 has sufficient torque capacity for big-blocks; it also came on some 351's. The C-4 has been standard on most small-blocks, sixes and some four-cylinders while the more recent C-3 is limited to four-cylinder engines. The FMX came with most 351's. The C-5 is basically a C-4 with a lock-up converter designed to give better mileage. Whichever you have, it is mandatory that you install a transmission oil cooler that does a far better job of cooling the transmission fluid than the stock oil cooler which is built into the radiator. Heat is the transmission's greatest enemy and you'll add thousands of miles to your transmission's life with this simple addition. There is an acceptable one in Ford's Motorsport Catalog and there are many other aftermarket coolers available as well.

One problem with the stock system is that should your engine overheat, it is quite likely that the transmission fluid will also overheat and be unable to perform its job. This, however, is rarely noticed and early transmission failure often occurs because the fluid isn't changed when the problem with engine overheating is dealt with. A transmission cooler will cool your transmission independent of the engine's own cooling system.

Besides the transmission cooler, the addition of a shift kit enables your transmission to shift more easily and adds to its life span. Both these procedures are easy to carry out.

Finally, I suggest changing the entire fluid every year or 15,000 miles if your Mustang is driven hard.

MANUAL TRANSMISSIONS

Pre-1974 Mustangs have either a version of the well-known Top Loader four-speed or a Borg-Warner T10 that was available on some early Mustangs and Shelbys. A three-speed manual was available as standard equipment on base and economy models. All these transmissions, especially the Top Loader, are strong designs. They can be left as they were originally turned out by the factory with the exception of the substitution of Hurst shifters which are far better than stock Ford units. Later Mustangs did not

A transmission oil cooler is recommended for all automatic transmissions. Photo courtesy Rudy Automotive.

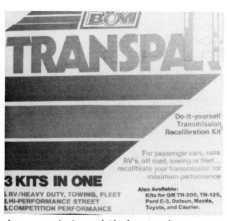

A transmission shift kit is also recommended. Photo courtesy Rudy Automotive.

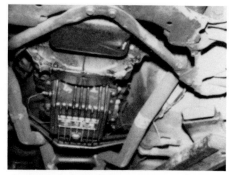

A transmission deep sump pan increases capacity and reliability. This is a B&M pan on a 1979 302 Mustang. Brad Davis photo.

use the beefy Top Loaders because the small four- and six- cylinder engines did not need such a strong transmission. The 1983 Mustangs got the Borg-Warner T-5 five-speed as an option, and it can handle the torque of a mildly modified 302. However, if you are putting a larger engine into your 1974 and later Mustang and want a strong transmission, you will have to adapt a Top Loader into it.

Most enthusiasts prefer to use aftermarket pressure plates and discs because they are of better quality. Factory pressure plates were made of cast iron bodies, which are not as strong as the steel aftermarket plates. There are many brands available but there is usually a problem when you install a higher-pressure plate. The Ford clutch linkage is already at its limit in terms of strength in stock form, and the use of an aftermarket plate necessitates beefing up the stock linkage or fabrication of new parts. The stock linkage will work for a very short while but will let you down at the worst possible place and time. I know.

It is a good idea to also use a safety bellhousing—it is lighter than some stock units and can contain an exploding clutch.

REAR AXLE

The 1973 and earlier Mustangs had either an eight- or nine-inch rear housing, both of which are strong enough to handle the torque of a modified

Hurst shifters, standard equipment on some Mustangs such as the 1970 Boss 302, are necessary for quick, accurate shifting. Steve Dowdall photo.

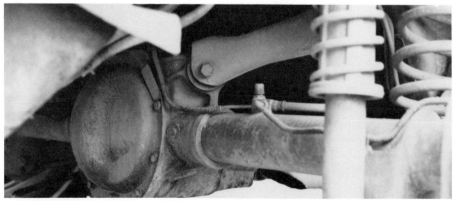

Newer Mustang rears aren't designed to handle the torque of a modified 302.

engine that came with the Mustang. The eight-inch rear, although strong, cannot handle drag-type starts (popping the clutch at 6500 rpm). The nine-inch is renowned for its strength and durability. The one to have is the one that uses a nodular iron case. This may or may not have a large letter N inscribed on it, but if your Mustang is a factory performance model, more likely than not it will have an N case, as do all the big-block 428 and 429 Mustangs. The big-blocks also have thicker axles, thirty-one-spline versus

A performance pressure plate, such as this Hays unit, is made of much better materials than stock units. Photo courtesy Hays Clutches.

A safety bellhousing has the ability to absorb a clutch or flywheel explosion. This is rare but when it does happen, the results are disastrous. Photo courtesy Lakewood Industries.

An N case rear is the one to have. Most will have the N letter, but some won't. Randy Ream photo.

twenty-eight-spline, for extra torque-handling capacity.

Most Mustangs also have a conventional or open differential. Under normal driving, power is evenly distributed to both rear wheels. However, with hard acceleration, cornering or slippery road surfaces, only one wheel grips the surface. This is not desirable in a performance Mustang. A limited slip rear distributes power equally to both wheels all the time and differential action is accomplished by clutch plate slippage within the differential. This is important in a performance Mustang because it results in better traction and cornering. In 1969, Ford introduced an improved limited slip design and called it Traction-Lok. This is the best type of differential to have in a street Mustang. Finally, some Shelby Mustangs and 1969-71 big-blocks had a Detroit Locker differential, which may be necessary in a race car, but it is noisy, expensive and not very practical for the street.

Regarding axle ratio selection, if you want acceleration, a 3.91 or 4.10 ratio is more than enough for the street. Going to a larger ratio really limits your Mustang's ability to cruise unless you have an overdrive or five-speed transmission. A good balance between acceleration and highway cruising is to pick a ratio between 3.25 and 3.50. Anything smaller will sacrifice acceleration. There are many ratios available for Ford's nine-inch rear; fewer for the eight-inch and 7½ inch rear.

The 1974 and later performance Mustangs got a 7½ inch rear. This is considered marginal for performance use, especially with the 302. Several suppliers (including Ford) offer a nine-inch conversion. This modification

This is a Traction-Lok differential. Randy Ream Photo.

This is a "pumpkin," which houses the ring and pinion. Because of Ford's design, the whole setup can be easily removed and replaced with another housing and different gear ratio. Randy Ream photo.

can be expensive but if you want the later Mustangs to perform, it is necessary. However, an eight-inch rear from a Maverick or early Mustang will also work after some alteration.

OTHER

If you can afford it, an oil cooler will help increase your engine's life and durability. Oil temperature should never go above 225°F, but even with an oil cooler it sometimes will. Temperatures over 275° F are dangerous, and 300°F is considered critical. The oil cooler that came on the Boss 429 and other Mustangs is a good design, good for about a thirty-degree drop in oil temperature.

It is wise to change your oil and filter every 2,000-2,500 miles. I am sure

There are many different gear ratios for the nine-inch rear. Randy Ream photo.

Used rears are available at swap meets. On the left is a nine-inch and on the right an eight-inch. The eight-inch can tolerate the torque of a modified small-block. The nine-inch can handle more than 500 hp in stock form with street tires.

you've noticed that many new car makers have recommended oil changes only every 7,500 or more miles. There are additives in most good oils that do not last beyond 2,000-2,500 miles; once they are gone, engine wear is accelerated. Stay with a particular brand and don't go too heavy on viscosity. If you use a multiviscosity oil, 20W-50 is a good choice. I don't recommend synthetic oils. They have a tendency to thin out at high rpm, resulting in the necessity of an immediate engine rebuild.

A modified Mustang requires more maintenance than a typical stock Mustang. Headers have a tendency of loosening up; weather changes affect carburetion and fine tuning is required. Keep everything clean so that you'll be able to spot potential trouble early, and at home. When something does go wrong, always, always check the simplest things first. Don't assume the problem is something major, or you may end up spending money for nothing. Part of the beauty of these machines is that with proper vigilance on your part, they can be enjoyed for many, many years.

An engine oil cooler will make the oil last longer and inhibit viscosity loss. This is a cooler that came on some 1969-71 Mustangs and it was good for a 30 degree drop in oil temperature.

CHAPTER 6

THE
2300
OHC FOUR

The smallest engine to be found in Mustangs since 1974 is the 2300 cc (140 cubic inches) inline overhead cam four. It has usually served as the base engine, and generally hasn't been enthusiastically received by street racers and hot rodders. After all, how much can you get out of 140 cubic inches, especially when larger V-8's are around? Like other engines, it can be made to perform better and the engine has some very interesting features, particularly the 2300 that powers the SVO Mustang.

The 2300, built to replace the Pinto's 2000 cc engine, was originally designed to share many parts with the 2000 to reduce cost. However, with new bore and stroke (3.781x3.126 inches) and bore spacing dimensions, this engine turned out to be different from the 2000, although they still share certain design similarities. For instance, both use a single overhead camshaft crossflow cylinder head for superior breathing. With a crossflow head, the intake manifold of the engine is located on one side and the exhaust manifold on the other side. The 2300 is also the first American-built engine using metric fasteners, requiring metric tools.

There is no doubt that the 2300 is a strong engine. It has a nodular iron crankshaft, supported by five two-bolt main bearings. Rods are forged steel and the stock bottom end is considered safe to at least 7000 rpm. Ford had some breakage problems with the 2000's camshaft, because it was supported by only three bearing pedestals. For the 2300, Ford used four pedestals for greater support.

In addition, the camshaft was rifle-drilled to provide oiling to the cam followers and valvetrain. This, unfortunately, was a problem on many 2300's. The cam followers were made of a metal that turned out to be too soft. Apparently, as the followers wear away, bits of metal plug the oiling passages on the camshaft, resulting in camshaft failure due to lack of oil. Ford lists a hydraulic cam with a 0.412 inch lift for the 2300 in the Motorsport Catalog. It is recommended that the stock cam be replaced with either this cam or, preferably, an aftermarket cam which has higher lift, to about 0.500 inch, as the 2300 likes more lift.

The 2300 uses intake valves measuring 1.73 inches and exhausts measuring 1.50 inches. The valves are canted in opposite directions to improve combustion and produce more horsepower. An unusual feature of the 2300's cylinder head design is the intake ports. You'll note that the two outer ports are oval in configuration while the inner two are round. In 1979, Ford made an additional change by altering the shape of all the ports to a D design. This was done to increase flow velocity and it is the recommended head for any kind of performance use. It was a running change, meaning that some 1979 engines have the older design while others have the D-port heads.

One anomaly of the 2300 cylinder head is that all four intake ports are different, even though at first glance it looks as if the two outer and the two inner ports are the same. This is not that important in a street engine, but if you ever race your 2300, a porting job will be necessary.

This all-out race 2300 shows the crossflow head design with the induction system on one side and the exhaust system on the other. Photo courtesy Racer Walsh.

1974-79 intake ports. Note canted valves and four pedestal cam supports.

1979 and later heads feature revised D ports for better flow.

Exhaust ports are round on all 2300's.

The stock 2300 engine will respond well to some simple modifications. The stock air cleaner is extremely restrictive, and simply replacing the stock air filter element with a taller one (so that the lid of the air cleaner is more than ¼ inch taller) results in a 25 cfm increase. It is wise, however, to replace the entire stock air cleaner with an efficient aftermarket unit.

The stock intake manifold, which looks efficient, is actually restrictive, limiting flow to the engine to about 250 cfm. This means that if you install a carburetor larger than stock, which flows about 225 cfm, all that extra capacity will be wasted.

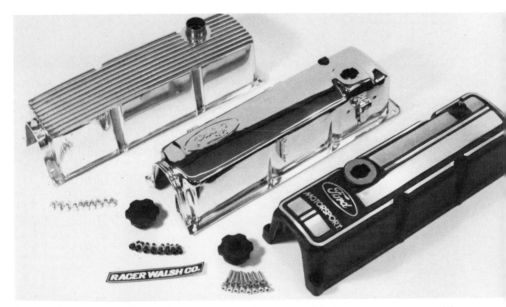

You can dress up your 2300 with one of these valve covers. Photo courtesy Racer Walsh.

Factory stock 2300. Fresh-air system helps but the stock air cleaner is very restrictive.

A good replacement is Offenhauser's dual-port intake manifold and a small Holley 390 cfm four-barrel carburetor. This combination is very popular as it provides good mileage and more than twenty-five horsepower over stock.

Changing the camshaft on the 2300 is not very difficult. A good guide to follow is to use slightly more duration than stock while increasing valve lift to 0.500 inch. For street use, you can retain the stock self-adjusting hydraulic pivot.

Stock carburetor is on the left, replacement Weber on the right. Photo courtesy Racer Walsh.

Difference is more obvious when turned upside down. Replacement Weber has larger venturis.

All 1974 and later Mustangs use a catalytic converter and a restrictive muffler. Use of exhaust headers and a good turbo muffler results in a 15 hp increase. This is a worthwhile increase and very cost effective, as the 2300 needs only a single exhaust system.

These simple modifications result in a 2300 that produces about 145 hp, not quite as much as a turbocharger system, but definitely much more reliable and a lot cheaper. And, as important, such engine modifications do not introduce any throttle lag in the engine, which is considered normal in a turbo application.

Ford has made two attempts to turbocharge the 2300. The first was in 1979. Unfortunately, in spite of precautions such as forged pistons and other improved and strengthened internal engine components, these

There is no shortage of intake manifolds for the 2300. These are all Offenhauser manifolds. Photo courtesy Racer Walsh.

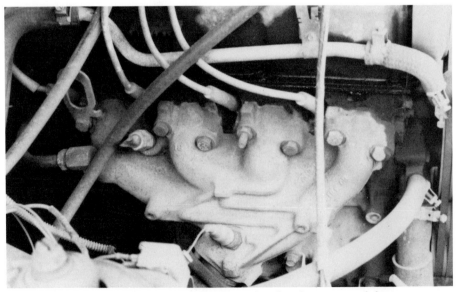

The stock exhaust manifold is not a bad design but headers are much better.

engines have had a high failure rate.

The 1984 SVO Mustang uses a better system incorporating fuel injection, variable computer-controlled electronic turbo boost and an air-to-air intercooler, to boost horsepower to 175. It is an expensive and complex system relying heavily on electronics and its modification is beyond the capability of most backyard mechanics. The 1985 version boasts 205 hp.

There are also several aftermarket turbo systems that provide reliable

For optimum street performance Offenhauser's four-barrel intake with a Holley 390 cfm carb is required. Photo courtesy Racer Walsh.

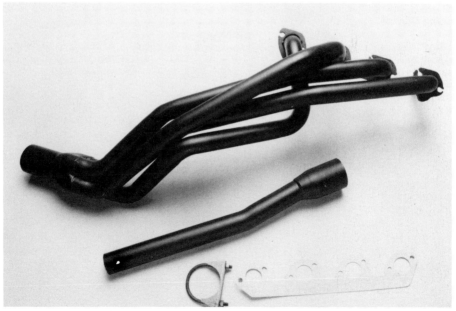

This tuned header is available from DOBI. Photo courtesy DOBI.

performance, but all these are expensive. Considering the cost of the bolt-on modifications and the horsepower increase, it is hard to justify spending so much on a 2300, considering how heavy Mustangs are. Even with turbocharging, a 2300 can't keep up with a mildly modified 302.

The 2300 is a good engine and its good points show up in racing. For the street, the 2300 will show itself well when Ford installs it in a lighter car.

This is the less than successful attempt at turbocharging on the 1979 Mustangs.

The 1984 SVO Mustang with a superior turbocharging system.

Besides the 1984 Turbo SVO, is the Turbo GT engine rated at 145 hp, which also features fuel injection. The engine is set back farther compared to the 1979 Turbo 2300.

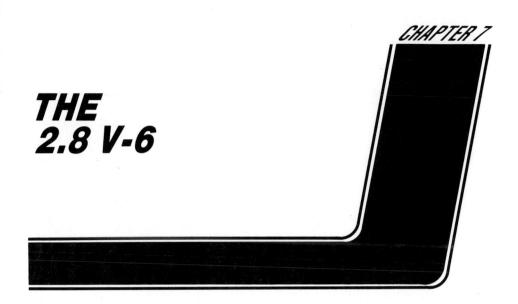

CHAPTER 7

THE
2.8 V-6

The Mustang II's and the 1979 Mustang were all available with the 2800 cc (171 cubic inches) V-6. It was designed to bridge the gap between the 2300 four-cylinder and the 302 V-8. With the V-6's extra twenty-five or so horsepower (depending on year), you could load up your Mustang with all the power options and still get some measure of get-up-and-go. This would have been very difficult with the four-cylinder.

The V-6, which also powered the German-built Capri, was imported from Germany for the Mustang. It has a bore of 3.66 inch and a stroke of 2.70 inch. A smaller version of this engine, the 2600 cc, powered the Capri during 1972-73. Although very similar, there are very important differences between the two engines. Internally, they are pretty much the same, with the exception of bore. The main difference is the cylinder heads. The 2800 engine has a separate exhaust port for each cylinder which results in better exhaust scavenging. The 2600 uses two ports with two cylinders sharing one port per head. The 2800 uses a nodular cast iron crankshaft and forged steel rods. In addition, the 2800 uses a mechanical camshaft, which requires periodic rocker arm adjustment.

Weighing in at 305 pounds, the V-6 is a small, compact engine with a very good reputation for reliability. In stock form, the small carburetor and camming can limit performance to about 5500 rpm. There the engine runs out of breath. In stock form, the 2800 is capable of 7000 rpm shifts with no problem; however, an aftermarket camshaft is required. The only sore point with this V-6 is its timing gears, which have a habit of shredding the nylon teeth during performance use. These should be replaced with an all-metal gear, such as the Cloyes unit.

There is not much available for this engine. Offenhauser has a dual-port intake manifold which should be used with a Holley 390 cfm carburetor. Headers (available from several manufacturers) are recommended, as are the usual ignition modifications. The Mustang's drivetrain can handle the

Stock V-6.

An all-metal cam gear assembly is required on the 2800, such as this Cloyes unit. Photo courtesy Rudy Automotive.

59

V-6's output so that swapping to a nine-inch rear and stronger transmission is not necessary.

This little engine has great potential. It's unfortunate that it has been passed over by Ford and the general enthusiast population.

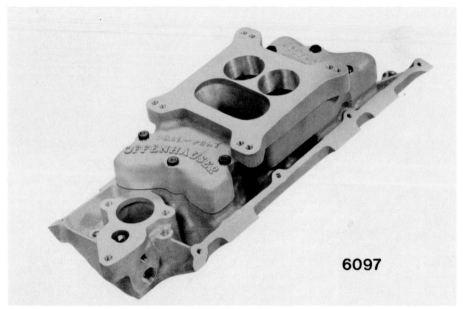

Offenhauser makes this dual-port intake for the 2800 and is recommended.

CHAPTER 8

THE 3.8 V-6

The newest engine producing power for the Mustang is the 3.8 (232 cubic inches) V-6. It has a bore and stroke of 3.682x3.126 and weighs 298 pounds, considerably less than GM's V-6's. The low weight is due to aluminum cylinder heads which feature Cleveland-type ports and good-size valves, measuring 1.77 inch intake and 1.45 inch exhaust. The valves, however, are not canted like the Cleveland engines, and are arranged in a conventional straight line.

In 1983, the first year this engine was available, it was rated at 112 hp with the use of a two-barrel carburetor. For 1984 the engine was upgraded with electronic fuel injection and was rated at 120 hp. One disadvantage in 1984 was that the only transmission available for the V-6 was the automatic overdrive (AOD).

It is still a little early for this engine to receive any attention from aftermarket manufacturers in relation to bolt-on equipment. The only "performance" parts that Ford sells for this engine are chrome valve covers.

If you own a Mustang with this engine, I suggest you limit modifications to the exhaust system. You could also mount a Holley carburetor in place of the stock Motorcraft unit or fuel injection, but I would wait until a performance intake manifold is made available for this engine.

With the high probability that Ford will drop the remaining V-8's from its engine lineup in the next few years, it is best to wait until further development work is done, especially in the areas of durability and reliability under performance use. It is quite likely that this 232 V-6 will become Ford's premier performance engine in the late eighties.

The 3.8 is a nice, compact engine with great potential. Note aluminum heads.

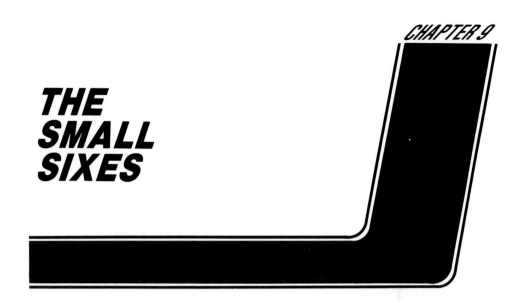

CHAPTER 9

THE SMALL SIXES

Ford's inline six-cylinder first appeared in 1960, to power the Falcon. The original displacement of this engine series was 144 cubic inches, but it was dropped in favor of the larger 170- and 200-cubic-inch versions. The 1964 Mustang had the 170-cubic-inch version, but by 1965, it was replaced by the slightly more powerful 200, more in keeping with the Mustang's image. The 200 continued as the standard Mustang engine until 1970 and made another appearance during 1979-82. The 250 was available from 1969-73.

Before going further, it should be mentioned that Ford produced another six-cylinder, a 240-cubic-inch, which was known as the Ford Big Six. It was based on the 223-cubic-inch inline six that has been standard with Ford since 1952. The 240, introduced in 1965, was phased out in 1972. This particular six was available only on the larger Ford cars, usually as the standard engine, and it was of a different engine family than the Small Six series. There is no interchangeability between the two engine families, and in typical Ford fashion, both 240 and 250 engines were available together in the same car line for a number of years, which confused the public. In addition, a 300-cubic-inch version of this engine was and is available on vans and other Ford utility vehicles. Because the Big Six had a conventional bolt-on intake manifold and better head design, it was more successful in racing and better-suited for performance modifications.

Over the years, the Small Six has proven itself to be a reliable, economical engine. It doesn't provide spectacular performance because it was not designed to. There is no performance version of this engine, either. Ford cars with this engine are usually good candidates for a V-8 engine swap. Those enthusiasts "stuck" with the six are not without hope, however, since this little engine can be modified to provide excellent low- to mid-range performance and, most important, at a very reasonable cost.

The 170-cubic-inch version has a bore and stroke of 3.50x2.94 and an important limitation of only four main bearings. The 200-inch measures 3.68x3.13 while the 250 has the same bore, but is further stroked to 3.91. Both the 200 and 250 have seven main bearings.

One of the biggest problems with the Small Six is harmonics, or vibration. Vibrations travel from the front of the crankshaft to the flywheel where they are returned to the front of the crank. This is normal with all engines. The problem is that the Small Six does not have a vibration dampener to absorb the vibrations, so the bearings, timing gears and even the flywheel can break when the engine is over-revved. That is why it is important not to exceed a limit of 5500-6000 rpm. In fact, it is best to stay around 5000 rpm for safety's sake.

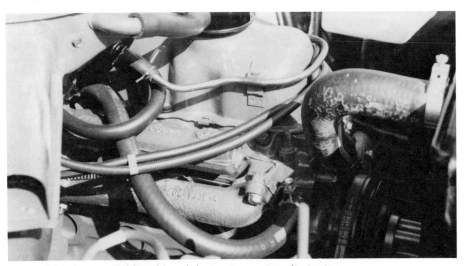

Integral intake manifold and head design is a serious limitation.

Small Six dressed up with an Offenhauser valve cover.

Probably its biggest limitation is the integral intake manifold/head design. The intake manifold is actually part of the cylinder head, and there is no factory performance intake manifold/head to fit this engine.

About the only aftermarket intake manifolds available for the Small Six are made by Offenhauser. Part number 5970 is designed to fit 1970 and later engines and it is a 3x1V setup. Installation requires removal of the cylinder head and some machining operations. Part number 5205 fits 1961-69 engines and requires similar machining. The three one-barrel carburetors provide more than enough fuel mixture to transform the engine into a performer.

Several years back, Ford expert Ak Miller got around the carburetion problem, but it is a lot of work. Basically, the ends of the intake manifold can be milled flat so that a carb adaptor can be used after a hole is drilled into the manifold. This way, 3x1V carbs can be used to boost horsepower.

There are also adaptors available to fit the stock intake manifold so that a larger two-barrel carburetor can be used. This modification will not improve performance substantially, because you can only get so much gas mixture through the stock one-barrel orifice. It does look good, though.

As with most Ford engines, big gains can be made by modifying the exhaust side of the Small Six. At the very least, the stock muffler can be replaced by a free-flowing one. For later Mustangs with catalytic converters, you can get one of those "test" pipes which really can make a big difference. Headers, of course, are much better, as these can increase power and economy dramatically.

Most Small Six engines come with a distributor that only has vacuum advance. Acceleration can be improved by using a Mallory distributor that has centrifugal advance.

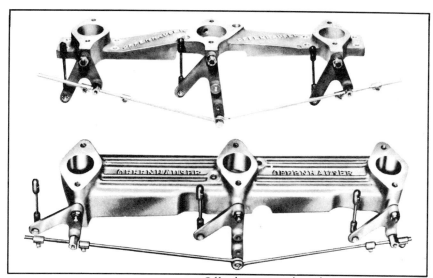

Offenhauser makes these two manifolds for the Small Six. Photo courtesy Offenhauser Sales Corporation.

It is often recommended to swap the 250 head on the 200 engine, which will result in some horsepower gain because the 250 has better valving. If you have a 200 engine and are looking for more power, it is better to swap a complete 250 engine instead of just the head. Fifty cubic inches and a longer stroke provide much more low end power than just a cylinder head change and, visually, the 200 and 250 are identical.

Speaking of swaps, a four-speed manual might be worthwhile for those having a three-speed manual. The only change required is to shorten the driveshaft to accommodate the longer four-speed Top Loader transmission. The 170 doesn't readily lend itself to this modification as the bellhousing, clutch and flywheel from a 200 or 250 will also have to be used. This applies to 1973 and earlier sixes.

The simple modifications outlined here (with the exception of the 3x1 carb setup) will result in a very torquey, low end performer. First-gear acceleration will take a lot of the "big boys" by surprise, and the six will still be able to deliver economical, reliable performance.

Installing a two-barrel on the stock manifold is a largely wasted exercise, as you can only get so much airflow through the stock manifold opening.

Typical modified Small Six with headers, Holley two-barrel and performance air cleaner.

CHAPTER 10

THE SMALL-BLOCKS

By far, Ford's small-block is the engine that most enthusiasts associate with the Mustang. In one form or another, this engine series has been the power behind every year of Mustang production, with the exception of 1974, when the V-8 was not available.

The first version of the small-block, a 221, made its debut in 1962. By 1964 it was bored out to 260 cubic inches and later to the well-known 289 cubic inches. Unlike previous Ford engines, the small-block was very compact and light, weighing in at 450 pounds. Its wide bore and short stroke design make it conducive to high rpm operation.

The 1964½ Mustang had a 260 version as its largest option, but by 1965, the 289 became the standard V-8. Four-barrel 289's were available only during 1965-67; a four-barrel 302 was available in 1968 and again in 1983-85. All the rest of the 289/302's were two-barrel engines.

There are two variants of the small-block that haven't been mentioned: The first is the Boss 302 engine which powered the Boss 302 Mustangs in 1969-70. It produced by far the highest output of all the production small-blocks. This engine is really a small-block with modified 351C cylinder heads. The other is the 351W (for Windsor), also introduced in 1969. It is basically an enlarged 302, yet there isn't much interchangeability, besides the cylinder heads, between it and other small-blocks.

With the small-block's tremendous and varied racing heritage, it is no surprise that there is available a wealth of both factory and aftermarket equipment to wake this engine up. The procedures are fairly straightforward, even if you want to build a copy of the 306 hp 289 that came in the 1965-67 Shelby. The 306 hp Shelby engine is in reality a built-up 271 hp Hipo 289. It has an aluminum high-rise intake manifold, 715 cfm Holley carb, steel tube exhaust headers, deep sump oil pan in addition to all the regular 271 hp 289 features. This amounts to a factory-hot-rodded engine.

289/302

To reach this stage, however, on a regular 289 or 302 will require some work. The 289 Hipo came with a lot of equipment as standard. It used special

306 hp remains the highest rating for a small-block. They came on 1965-67 Shelby Mustangs.

Stock 2V 289 was rated at 200 hp in 1967.

forged rods with ⅜ inch rod bolts, screw-in rocker studs, a solid lifter camshaft, dual-point distributor, special high rpm balancer and free-flowing exhaust manifolds. The reason for all this equipment was to make sure the engine would live at higher rpm. Ford could have made the engine put out more horsepower but it didn't, as evidenced by the rather restrictive stock cast iron intake manifold and small 480 cfm carburetor. The enthusiast was supposed to take over from where Ford left off.

The bulk of 289/302 engines installed in Mustangs were two-barrel, single exhaust engines. The steps to improve output and performance are fairly straightforward. For best results a free-flowing dual exhaust system with turbo-type mufflers is necessary. Because the small-block is a compact engine, installing headers does not pose much difficulty, as there is plenty of

A necessary expense on the small-block is to convert to an adjustable valvetrain so that a high-performance camshaft can be used. At left is shown stock pressed-in rocker studs while the Hipo head on the right uses screw-in rocker studs.

271 hp 289 was a high point in small-block history. This one has a high-rise intake and Holley carb.

room on all small-block-equipped Mustangs. The stock two-barrel intake manifold should be replaced by an aluminum four-barrel intake along with a Holley 600 cfm carburetor. There are many manifolds to choose from. If you prefer to stay with a factory design, the well-known Cobra manifold is available. If you want more power without sacrificing low end response,

An eighties performance small-block. They still don't make as much horsepower as the sixties versions, but they are slowly getting there. This 1984 302 is rated at 175 hp.

This is a well-prepared 289. X-type single plane intake manifold, headers and a mild cam provide impressive performance from 289 cubic inches.

there are many X-type single-plane manifolds to choose from. Either way, a good intake manifold/carburetor combination is worth at least 35-40 hp over stock.

The next area to consider is the camshaft. The 289 Hipo solid-lifter camshaft has been popular with Ford enthusiasts, but there are many after-market hydraulic grinds that work just as well, if not better, and do not require any maintenance. In any case, the stock timing chain must be replaced with a double-roller setup for greater reliability at high rpm. Even

Some impressive intake manifold setups for the small-block include this 2x4V (top) and this Weber 4x2V setup (bottom).

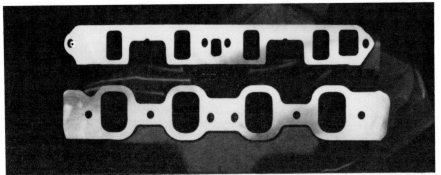

Intake port sizing is obvious from a comparison of 351W and 351C-4V intake manifolds.

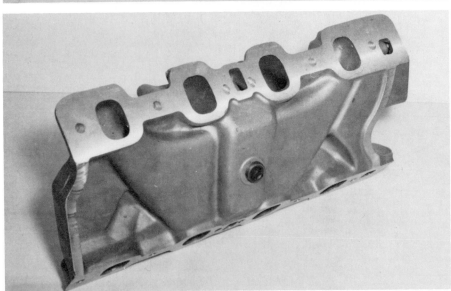

With the use of this intake manifold, bolting 351C-2V heads on your small-block is feasible. Photo courtesy B&A Ford Performance.

with hydraulic cams, it is a good idea to modify the cylinder heads to accept screw-in rocker studs, and guide plates that allow you to adjust the valves.

The small-block has an excellent oiling system. For high-performance use it is worthwhile to use a high-volume oil pump, the Boss 302 windage tray (C9ZZ-6687-B) and a deep sump oil pan. It is interesting to note that, in 1970, Ford revised oil dipstick levels on the Boss 302 so that an additional two quarts are added to the oil pan. Obviously, any high-performance small-block would benefit from increased oil capacity, but it is better to install a larger oil pan than to put an additional two quarts in the stock system.

If you really want to transform your small-block into a screamer, you can now install 351C two-barrel heads on any 289/302. These heads have the distinction of being readily available at junkyards at very low prices, and they outflow even modified 289/302 heads. Valves on the 351C heads measure intake at 2.04 inches and exhaust, 1.65 inches, already bigger than the biggest valves that can be fitted on the stock heads or 351W heads. The ports are superior, too. However, be careful when choosing 351C used heads, as some are prone to cracking. This problem shows up on engines that have overheated. Be sure to have them thoroughly checked out. There are some other modifications required for this swap but all the information is available from the manufacturer that made this possible, B&A Ford Performance.

Exhaust ports on the 351W (top) are small when compared to the Boss 302/351C-4V exhaust ports (bottom).

Intake ports (top) on the 351C-2V head and exhaust ports (bottom) are much more reasonable for good street performance, especially when used on the 289/302 small-block. These are Australian versions, which have the smaller, quench 4V combustion chamber.

1979 and later 302's use this serpentine belt system. You can gain an easy 20 hp if you use Kaufmann Products' underdrive engine pulley kit, which consists of three pulleys, while retaining stock belt system.

Without the intake manifold that B&A manufactures, it would not be possible to install these heads on the regular 289/302.

A properly built conversion will outperform the Boss 302 engine on the street. For all intents and purposes, this conversion amounts to a Boss 302 engine with Cleveland 2V heads, which is a better combination than the overly large ports on the stock Boss 302.

There has been quite a bit written about installing 351W heads on the 289/302. This modification results in about a 7 hp gain, because the 351W has slightly larger intake valves and ports, although the exhaust ports are smaller. It is not a significant increase considering the effort required.

Many 302 heads have very restrictive exhaust ports due to a large Thermactor boss cast in the port. These should be ground away to get any kind of performance from the 302.

Regarding ignition, the recommendations made in the ignition chapter should be followed.

255

This version of the small-block was available on Mustangs during 1980-

The 1985 302 HO (referred to by Ford as 5.0 HO-4V) benefits from factory roller lifters, roller timing chain, higher compression, tube headers, an accessory drive system that operates at two speeds and the air conditioning turns off at wide-open throttle. Coupled with a free-flowing factory exhaust system (40 percent less backpressure), this 302 pumps out an honest 210 hp at 4600 rpm.

82 as a replacement for the 302. Externally similar to the 302, intensive modifications are not recommended for this little V-8. It has been considerably lightened internally and the engine lacks the necessary strength to cope with extra horsepower. Mild exhaust system modifications are recommended.

There is no reason you can't retain creature comforts such as air conditioning with a high-performance 289.

The 351W is basically a stretched small-block.

351W

Although physically larger than the 302, it is considered a small-block. By increasing the stroke to 3.5 inches, the block's height was raised by one inch to accommodate the longer stroke. At the same time, the crank journals were resized, resulting in a small-block engine that has no interchangeability with other small-blocks, save the heads. However, restrictive porting and valves for an engine this size limit performance to low- to mid-range rpm.

After many years of having no aftermarket intake manifold available, now there are several available for the 351W. A good carburetor for this engine is Holley's list number 1850 flowing 600 cfm. Automatic transmission cars should use list number 4462.

Until recently, there weren't many intake manifolds available for the 351W. At top is an Offenhauser 360-degree manifold, while the bottom is a Holley single plane.

The 351W is a good design, but in stock or modified form a comparably modified 351C runs circles around it. However, it is interesting to note that the latest 351 SVO racing cylinder block is based on the 351W and not the 351C. The 351W is stronger and has a better oiling system.

BOSS 302

This is the ultimate and short-lived development of the small-block. The Boss 302 is another of those engines that is almost complete (from the

The Boss 302 small-block is still the strongest of all small-blocks, producing an actual 325 hp.

Boss 302 is the high point in small-block development. This is a 1969 version which features larger (2.23 versus 2.19 in 1970) intake valves. Randy Ream photo.

modification point of view) just as it came from the factory. Solid lifter cam, high-rise aluminum intake manifold and Holley 780 cfm carburetor, four-bolt main reinforced block, forged crank and rods and a dual-point distributor were all part of the package. The heart of the Boss 302 is the cylinder heads, basically modified 351C-4V heads using screw-in rocker studs, adjustable rockers and guide plates. Ports and valves are a bit too big for

The reason for the Boss 302's phenomenal output is the canted valve cylinder heads.

Occasionally, you may see a Boss 302 with the rare Cross Boss manifold and inline carb. Superiority for street use is questionable.

good street operation, but that was the way Ford designed engines back then.

A set of exhaust headers and a better exhaust system along with a modern electronic ignition are all that this engine really needs. Otherwise, there is very little reason to go into the engine except, of course, to replace the stock pistons which are guaranteed to crack between 10,000 and 30,000 miles. If you want more power you could use the SVO single-plane intake manifold, part number M-9424-B302, which is designed to make about 50 hp more than stock. It is a competition manifold so it would be wiser to install a small Holley Double Pumper, either a 600 or 650 cfm unit rather than the stock 780.

CHAPTER 11

THE
351
CLEVELAND

Ford's most modern V-8, and probably the best in terms of power output for its size, was in Mustangs from 1970-73. The "hot" 351C's were around for a very short time, 1970-71. Later Clevelands were not high performance in the sixties sense, yet all have the same potential.

It is the cylinder head design that makes the engine what it is and the 351C has the best-designed heads of any factory Ford V-8, short of a true hemi (such as the Boss 429 and sohc 427). It is true that Chevrolet pioneered the canted valve head design but Ford further refined it. From this standpoint, the only shortcoming of the stock Cleveland head is poor exhaust-port configuration but this doesn't affect street performance and is only a consideration on all-out race 351C's.

Unlike the 351W and the other small-blocks, the 351C was designed with two separate cylinder heads, known as the 2V and 4V heads. The more common 2V head has smaller ports and valves (2.04 intake, 1.65 exhaust), and nonadjustable rocker arms. All 2V heads have an open combustion chamber design for low compression and emission reasons.

4V heads have larger ports and valves (2.19 intake, 1.71 exhaust). The 1970-71 4V heads have closed or quench-type combustion chambers and nonadjustable rocker arms. All 1972-73 4V heads are identical, except that they now share the same open combustion chamber head design as the 2V heads.

Boss 351 heads for 1971 use screw-in studs and guide plates, as do the Boss 302's. The rocker arms were specially hardened, the springs were

81

heavier and the retainers and valves used single groove keepers. The heads were also machined a little differently to accommodate larger valve springs. Combustion chambers were the smaller quench type for higher compression. In 1972, Ford continued building the Boss 351 on a very limited basis, but called it the 351-HO. The heads were identical; however, the HO engine now had the larger combustion chambers for lower compression. Like the Boss 302, the Boss 351 and 351-HO were very complete packages. Little, if

The 351C-4V engine has powered thousands of Mustangs from 1970-73. It has excellent hop-up potential, as do all 351C engines.

The ultimate factory configuration of the 351C is the Boss 351 which was standard equipment on 1,806 Boss 351 Mustangs.

anything, more was needed to make these engines run, as witnessed by the Boss 351's quarter-mile times: low fourteens to high thirteens in a Mustang weighing close to 3,800 pounds.

There are some additional differences between the 2V and 4V engines, particularly the 4V's four-bolt mains. However, according to most sources, this doesn't make much difference on the street in terms of strength and reliability.

Much has been written about the 351C's oiling problems, and how to

Renamed 351-HO for 1972, the Boss 351 engine was detuned to 275 hp by using 4V open-chamber heads, a lower compression ratio (9.2) and a milder mechanical camshaft.

The 351C-2V heads are far more common, yet for the street, they provide excellent performance and better low end response than the larger-ported 351C-4V heads. Photo courtesy B&A Ford Performance.

cure them. This holds true for an all-out race engine, but doesn't apply to street engines. However, as with other Ford engines, it is always a good idea to install a deep sump oil pan.

It really doesn't take much to make the 351C come alive. The usual intake, exhaust and ignition modifications are all that is needed. 2V engines need a better hydraulic camshaft, as do the 351CJ and other 4V versions. The Boss 351 could use a more efficient carburetor, such as a Holley 750 cfm Double Pumper and headers for best performance.

As the bulk of 351C's have the 2V heads, there is no point in trying to hunt down a set of 4V heads to gain better performance, because the 2V heads are just as good, if not better. If you are planning to install a better cam, it is also a good idea to upgrade these heads to accept adjustable rocker arms. This requires some machining and investment. The rocker arm pedestals have to be machined and tapped for 7/16 studs; this procedure is shown in the latest Ford Motorsport Equipment Catalog. The parts needed are: rocker stud, M-6527-A311; rocker arm, M-6564-A322; guide plate, C9ZZ-6A564-A; pushrod, M-6565-A342. Stock rocker arms are known for their weakness and must be replaced. Changing to adjustable rocker arms enables you to use an aftermarket camshaft with higher lift. The only other weakness in the 2V head is the multigroove valve keepers. These are ok for street use with a hydraulic cam, but are not recommended for racing or a solid lifter cam.

Like other Ford engines, the 351C suffers from restrictive manifolding. If your Mustang doesn't have a good dual exhaust system, get one. A lot of magazine articles recommend a 2½-inch-diameter system. This is fine if you can afford it, but for street use, the factory dual exhaust with turbo mufflers is adequate. Headers, of course, make a big difference. Installation in the later big Mustangs is relatively easy because they have very roomy engine compartments.

Regarding induction, the Boss 351 aluminum intake is often recommended. However, aftermarket manufacturers have single-plane designs for both 2V and 4V heads which are better than the stock and Boss 351 dual-plane intakes. Most aftermarket intakes use the standard Holley carb bolt

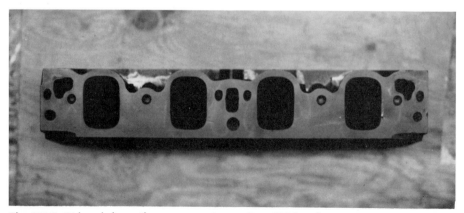

The 351C-4V heads have the same porting as Boss 302 heads.

pattern flange which should be no problem to install, as the stock carburetor is usually replaced at the same time. The 1971 351CJ and the other 1972-73 4V engines use a spreadbore-design carburetor which will not fit on Holley flange manifolds. (This is only relevant if you are interested in retaining the factory carb.)

Although Holley 600 cfm carbs are readily available and give excellent response, they are a bit small for a modified 351C. Holley list number 4118 flows 725 cfm (and accommodates Ford's automatic-transmission kick-down rod) and is a good choice. You can also use the 735 cfm that came on the 428CJ engine, which is usually available from Ford part vendors. I don't recommend Holley's 3310 750 cfm universal model. It doesn't quite work as well as it should. Manual-transmission Mustangs should use a Double Pumper in the 650-750 cfm range.

These simple modifications enable your 1970-73 Mustang to perform like a big-block without the weight penalty associated with a big-block.

Headers are necessary to bring out the most from your 351C. This one also has a Holley carburetor and factory ram air. Brad Davis photo.

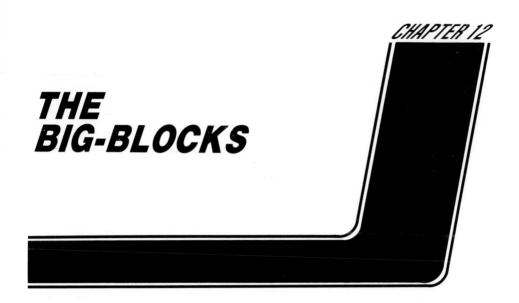

CHAPTER 12

THE BIG-BLOCKS

In 1967, Ford installed the big-block 390 in the Mustang. At the same time, Shelby installed the 428 (a bored and stroked 390) in the Shelby Mustang and called it the GT500. These engines were to propel the Mustang into the supercar class because of the enormous torque and horsepower they were capable of delivering. This was especially true for the 428's; the 390 could use some help.

Putting a big-block in the Mustang had the effect of changing the feel of the car. With the small-blocks, the Mustang felt light and nimble, but with 300 extra pounds over the front wheels, the big-block Mustangs tended to lose some of that sports car feel and developed traction problems. There was too much weight up front and too much torque for the rather skinny tires of the late sixties. These problems can be dealt with but the main problem is the 390, which didn't live up to its expectations.

390

The 390, with a bore of 4.05 inches and a stroke of 3.78 inches, was called the 390GT in 1967 and 1968. Although they were basically identical engines, they were rated at 320 and 325 hp respectively. In 1969, the 390 was again rated at 320 hp. Remember, these horsepower figures were gross; actual net figures were probably in the 260-265 hp range. Compression ratio was 10.5.

In spite of the GT nomenclature, the 390GT wasn't really a performance engine. Two-bolt mains, cast iron crank, very restrictive manifolding and a good hydraulic cam with very weak valve springs tended to reduce mid- and upper-rpm horsepower. It did have a 600 cfm Holley carburetor, but because of its deficiencies it ran out of breath at about 4000-4500 rpm. In the 1969 version, the Holley carburetor was replaced by an Autolite unit and the camshaft was downgraded to the standard 2V cam. The 390GT's cam was the same as used in the 428CJ/SCJ.

However, with so many cubic inches, any performance modifications made are amplified. The usual exhaust system modifications are helpful, as all 1967-69 390 Mustangs used the restrictive single-transverse-muffler setup. An aluminum intake manifold is also recommended. Ford made an abundance of intake manifolds for this engine series (the FE), and most are still available from Ford part vendors.

A good candidate is the aluminum intake from the 428 Police Interceptor engine which improves horsepower. The same manifold was used on the 428CJ except it was cast in iron. The most refined single four-barrel intake from Ford is the "sidewinder" intake, part number C6AZ-9424-M. The carburetor on this manifold is offset to the left in order to equalize fuel distribution. Of course, the aftermarket manufacturers make single-plane X-type manifolds for the big-block. An important advantage when switching to an aluminum intake is the weight savings. The stock cast iron intake weighs more than 100 pounds, whereas the typical aluminum intake should save fifty to sixty pounds, all off the front wheels.

In the ignition department, the usual recommendations apply. Recurve the distributor, replace the stock coil, and, if possible, convert to a modern electronic ignition system.

The stock 390GT cam is of a fairly good design. To get more rpm from the 390 all you have to do is install heavier valve springs, such as those found on the 428CJ or any good aftermarket spring. It is important to observe an

Big 390 mill first saw service in 1967. This is a 1969 version which has a milder camshaft and Autolite carburetor. In spite of these deficiencies, Ford rated it at 320 hp, the same as the 1967 390GT, which used a better cam and Holley 600 cfm carb.

rpm limit of 5500-6000 because above this point the engine's inherent oiling problems become evident. They are easy to fix, but require engine removal. The oil passage from the oil pump to the oil filter must be enlarged to ½ inch diameter and the restriction cast in the main oil gallery must also be enlarged. (This is located at the back of the block.) Your 390 should also have the larger, 427-type (COAZ-6881-A) oil filter adaptor. A windage tray (M-6687-A390) is a good, inexpensive addition. Finally, a high-volume, high-pressure pump (M-6600-A3) and oil pump pressure kit (M-6670-A390) are also necessary. As with other Ford engines, the addition of a deep sump oil pan is highly beneficial. These modifications are required on all 390/428 engines that are expected to rev over 6000 rpm and live.

428-428CJ

The 390 and, moreso, the 428 are ideal engines for Mustang enthusiasts who favor brute acceleration. There is nothing wrong with that, and these

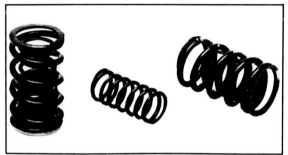

Your 390 will never realize its potential unless the stock valve springs are changed to allow the engine to rev over 5000 rpm.

While the Mustangs got the 390 in 1967, the Shelby Mustangs got a modified version of the Police Interceptor 428 using two 600 cfm Holley carburetors. Very impressive!

big-blocks can also be made to handle.

One of Ford's best street engines, the 428CJ, made its debut late in the 1968 model year. It featured the following: larger valves (2.09 inch intake,

The 428CJ and 428SCJ (which had stronger Le Mans-type rods) continued to be available through the 1970 model year. This is a ram-air version. Owner has installed a lighter, aluminum intake manifold.

The 428CJ first released in mid-1968 provided terrific performance.

1.65 inch exhaust), larger intake ports, a cast iron copy of the 428PI intake manifold, the 390GT cam, a 735 cfm Holley carburetor, rods with larger rod bolts, a windage tray and 10.6 compression. Beneficial modifications would include a better, freer-flowing dual exhaust system; headers; electronic ignition; and, to get rid some of that front end weight, an aluminum intake manifold. With so much power, there really isn't much need for a better camshaft or a larger carburetor.

There remain two other 428's to consider. First is the 428SCJ (Super Cobra Jet). It was identical to the 428CJ with the exception that it had 427 Le Mans-type rods. Mustangs with this engine got a mandatory oil cooler and rear axle ratios of 3.91 or 4.30.

The second is the 428 put in the 1967 and 1968 Shelby Mustang GT500's. The 1967 version was a 428 Police Interceptor engine with a dual-quad aluminum intake manifold setup—probably a little too much carburetion for a street engine, but very impressive to look at. It was rated at 355 hp. In 1968, the engine reverted to a more conventional single four-barrel Holley, yet was rated at 360 hp. Modification guidelines are the same as for the 390 and 428CJ.

427

The only other FE big-block that came in the Mustang was the 427 Low Riser, available for a short time in 1968. (A few 427 Medium Risers were sneaked through on some 1967 Shelbys.) It featured the superior side-oiler block for much improved oiling, but other than that, it wasn't much different

If you have the time, patience and money, it is possible to have a streetable big-block with Weber carbs.

than the 428CJ that replaced it. The heads were identical and camshaft events were the same, but it did have a smaller 600 cfm Holley carburetor. Because of the 427's wider bore and shorter stroke (4.23x3.78) it tended to produce its power at a higher rpm, which is not advantageous in a street car. In addition, it could only be ordered with an automatic transmission, which some consider a disadvantage, and it was also a very expensive option, which accounts for its rarity today.

429CJ-429SCJ

Ford's most modern big-block, the 385 Series, made its debut in 1968 but it wasn't until 1971 that it was installed in the Mustangs. From a design point of view, it is basically a large 351C. It has an identical oiling system and the cylinder heads have the same configuration. The 429CJ installed in the Mustang has four-bolt mains in the 2, 3, and 4 positions; a hydraulic camshaft; extremely large valves (2.25 intake, 1.72 exhaust); and intake ports that rival those found on the Boss 429 engine. The 429CJ uses a GM Rochester Quadrajet carburetor rated at 700 cfm.

The 429SCJ, in addition to the items listed for the 429CJ, has a mechanical camshaft, adjustable rockers and guide plates, and a larger Holley 780 cfm carburetor. It was also rated at 375 hp, five more than the 429CJ. Both are meaningless figures since each engine produced easily over 400 hp.

One of the reasons for the 428CJ's performance is that it used 427 Low-Riser heads (top) which have larger ports and valves than the regular 428 head (bottom).

Although much like the 428CJ, the 429's provide excellent street performance but have their share of problems. Considering the valves and porting, which can be considered superior to the FE Series, the engine requires some work to provide the power expected from it. The cylinder heads have intake ports that are too large for good street operation. Ports

A popular intake for the FE Series is this sidewinder intake manifold. This and other manifolds are usually to be found at swap meets and through part vendors who sell used Ford engine parts.

This is an example of a "radical" big-block Mustang, using a 429. All that carburetion is wasted with stock exhaust manifolds.

The 429CJ and 429SCJ were supposed to be introduced in the 1970 Mustang but introduction was delayed until the 1971 model. Although it has a large engine, the 1971 Mustang is roomier, relative to earlier big-block Mustangs.

that size are optimum for a much larger engine; at that time, before the oil crisis, Ford had plans of releasing a 501-cubic-inch version. Modifying the base 429 heads, which have smaller ports and valves,to work with an adjustable valvetrain will result in a much more responsive and powerful street 429. In addition, the exhaust ports on the 429's need some porting to remove cast-in obstructions and the Thermactor boss.

The 429 is a big, heavy engine, approaching a weight of 800 pounds. It would be wise to install an aluminum intake manifold, not only to improve

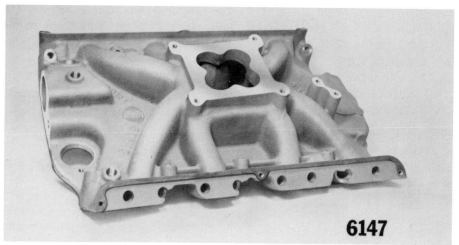

For a more up-to-date design, Offenhauser's Port-O-Sonic is a good choice. Photo courtesy Offenhauser Sales Corporation.

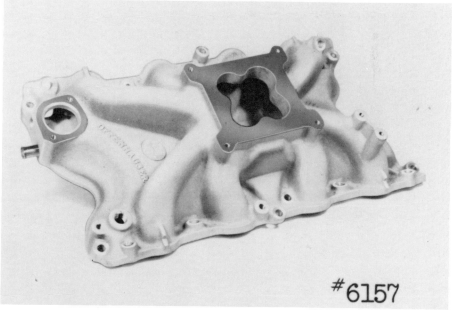

The best aftermarket intake manifold for the 429 is Offenhauser's Port-O-Sonic. Photo courtesy Offenhauser Sales Corporation.

power but to shed some of that weight. The best single four-barrel intake for this engine is Offenhauser's Port-O-Sonic. Although it is made for the smaller port base heads, there is enough material around the port to allow matching to the larger 429CJ ports.

The 429 uses the same oiling system as the 351C engine. It can use some minor modifications. The oil passage from the oil pump to the oil filter should be increased to ⅝ inch, and to ensure that the engine will have enough oil at rpm over 6000, a deep sump oil pan is necessary. Milodon makes a pan and pickup to fit the 429.

Both 429CJ and 429SCJ have cams that are suitable for high-performance street use. It is also very easy to change to an adjustable valvetrain on the 429CJ. All that is needed is new rocker arm studs (M-6527-A311) and rockers (M-6564-A322).

As with other Ford engines, the ignition should be updated. Since the 429 uses the same distributor as the 351C, there is no shortage of replacements for this engine.

BOSS 429

This is the ultimate production version of the 429, made only in 1969-70 so that Ford could race the engine in National Association for Stock Car Automobile Racing (NASCAR) events. It has aluminum dry-deck (no head gasket) cylinder heads with a modified hemi-design combustion chamber. Ports are large, and the heads have even larger valves than the 429CJ, measuring 2.28 intake and 1.90 exhaust. Other features include a forged steel crankshaft, large six-quart oil pan, aluminum intake manifold, adjust-

Boss 429 is the ultimate street big-block.

able rocker arms, 735 cfm Holley carburetor and hydraulic cam (1970 engines used the 429SCJ mechanical cam).

This engine has all the right pieces, yet to produce the kind of power that it was designed to produce, the Boss 429 owner is encouraged to change the camshaft, install stiffer valve springs and use a larger Holley carburetor. Boss 429's are notorious for spun bearings, a result of the insufficient capacity of the oiling system. Installing a deep sump oil pan usually cures the oil starvation problems that occur if the engine is revved over 6000 rpm.

In addition, an engine with such large ports and valves requires a better exhaust system. Headers are available for the Boss 429 and the ones made by JR Headers are recommended. Installation is difficult.

Another problem for the Boss 429 owner who wants to change intake manifolds (besides the lack of readily available manifolds) is that a water

Headers are a very tight fit on the Boss 429 Mustang. The best design is this made by JR Headers.

manifold has to be fabricated. Most performance manifolds available for the Boss 429 are actually race manifolds that have been adapted for street use. These do not have provision for a thermostat, thus the water manifold. However, the stock high-rise manifold is adequate for best all-around use, along with a Holley 800 Double Pumper.

These simple modifications transform the Boss 429 into a reliable street screamer with fantastic upper-rpm acceleration.

This Boss 429 has the rare race Torque Box intake manifold which requires the use of a fabricated water manifold and a special tall distributor. Note large Holman & Moody NASCAR air cleaner.

Here is another race manifold adapted for street use, using two Holley carburetors. This is a case where extra carburetion actually helps street performance because the manifold features much smaller ports than other Boss 429 intake manifolds. Thus velocity and flow at low speeds is maintained.

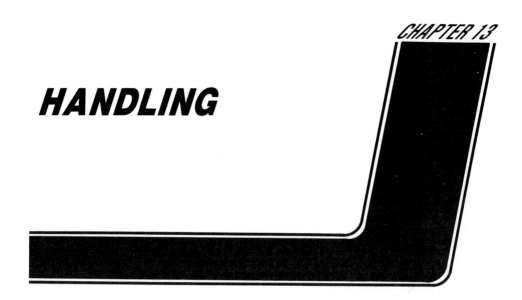

CHAPTER 13

HANDLING

Handling is a vast and sometimes complicated subject, yet handling boils down to just one thing: traction. This doesn't mean just cornering; handling involves all facets of driving—during acceleration, braking and cornering under all types of conditions and on all road surfaces. Another way of looking at it is that handling means control and predictability. A good-handling car will be fun to drive fast, while one that doesn't handle well will not only be difficult to drive, it will be unsafe and dangerous. A good-handling car should be controllable and should also provide a good degree of riding comfort, which will necessitate some compromise.

Compared to today's Mustangs, the performance Mustangs of the 1964-73 era were all strong (depending on engine) in terms of acceleration. In handling, the early Mustangs were as good as their competition, which by today's criteria could surely be improved upon. The 1974-78 Mustang II was not initially designed for performance, but in the later years of production, effort was made by Ford to improve the II's image. The 1979 and later Mustangs were designed to handle better than their predecessors, yet even the high-performance models still need some owner modification to bring them up to the level of Mustang's street competition. This even applies to the high touted SVO Mustang.

The guidelines in the following pages are aimed at preserving a balance among the qualities that constitute good handling while maintaining a reasonable ride. The enthusiast who is concerned with performance is usually willing to give up some ride quality but it is unwise to go overboard and sacrifice driveability and comfort. Particular attention will be paid to keeping costs down and limiting modifications to those within the reach of the average enthusiast on a limited budget. This will mean limiting modifications to bolt-ons. Extreme suspension modifications are reserved for race-only Mustangs and are beyond the scope of this book.

In order to achieve a better understanding of handling, particularly cornering, an explanation of some terms is included. Rather than go too deeply into a highly technical and difficult-to-understand explanation, this section will be immediately followed by a list of factors that affect handling and suggestions to make Mustangs handle to their capacity.

UNDERSTEER, OVERSTEER

A car, as it approaches and enters a turn, would rather continue going straight because of centrifugal force. In a front-heavy car (all Mustangs), additional loads placed on the front tires during a turn make the car begin to slide. In order to continue turning, the driver cranks in more steering to compensate. Going too fast at the corner will result in the car sliding off the road, unless the driver lets off the gas or turns the other way. If the driver continues to try to make a turn, at the limit of adhesion, he has a situation of valiantly trying to add more turning angle as the car leaves the road. This understeer is considered safe by Detroit, because the driver reacts instinctively, letting off the gas and turning away from the turn.

In an oversteering situation, the opposite occurs. The car enters the turn and, as soon as centrifugal force affects the car, the rear tires slide more than the front tires so the car turns tighter than the amount of steering input. Deliberate suspension design and a rear weight bias causes this. If not corrected, the car continues making a tighter turn. At the limit of adhesion, the car spins to the inside, with the driver turning the wheel away from the turn to try to save the situation.

Slight oversteer is preferred for racing because a skilled driver can control the car more easily and corner faster.

With most Mustangs, what we have is initial understeer followed by terminal oversteer at the limit of adhesion—essentially, both ends of the car losing traction.

Driving a car that understeers or oversteers excessively is too much work. That is why the installation of a rear sway bar on Mustangs, while adding oversteer, decreases understeer and makes driving more fun. Ford's philosophy, with very few exceptions, was to design lots of understeer into the Mustang chassis and this, in spite of the current emphasis on handling, has occurred in the newest 1979 and later Mustangs. Listed below are four steps or procedures that you can take to reduce understeer in your Mustang:

1. Increase front tire/wheel size
2. Stiffen rear springs
3. Increase front tire pressure
4. Increase rear sway bar diameter

TIRES

Tires, obviously, are the most important factor in handling—they are the only link the car has with the road.

From a handling point of view, the most important feature in choosing a particular tire is its ability to grip the road. The tire's contact patch actually interlocks with small irregularities on the surface of the road. Increase the size of this interlocking area or contact patch and, generally speaking, you get greater grip and thus better handling. When the tire slips or slides, such as in hard acceleration, the interlocked rubber is ripped off the tire, resulting in skid marks.

Wheel rim size affects a tire's ability to grip the road. A wider-than-stock rim reduces the tire's side flexibility, thus reducing distortion which enables the tire to grip better. Like everything else, there is an optimum wheel size for a particular tire size and choosing a tire wider than the manufacturer's recommendations will hurt handling.

Picking a tire for your Mustang can be difficult. The market is loaded with many different brands, types and prices. During the past few years, it seems that most tire manufacturers frequently come out with new and improved versions (usually more costly) of their top-of-the-line street tires. One thing is certain: Stay away from the cheap, bargain-basement tires. These aren't meant to hold up during any kind of performance (fast) driving.

The 1964-73 Mustangs came with either bias-ply or belted bias-ply tires. (Radials were optional since 1969). Bias refers to the type of construction used in the tire. The cords in a bias-ply tire are criss-crossed across the tire, from bead to bead. Bias-ply tires are usually the cheapest to manufacture and are the ones that have been around for years. They are quiet and provide a comfortable ride.

Belted tires are constructed similar to bias-ply tires, but with a belt (usually fiberglass) under the tread surface. This reduces tread distortion. Belted tires were considered the ultimate in the late sixties. They are considerably better than bias-ply tires but do not fare as well when compared to a modern radial.

You can manage to fit a large, modern radial in early Mustangs such as this GT350H. This Goodyear Eagle ST uses a fiberglass belt rather than steel.

The high point in the early Mustang tire technology was these Goodyear Polyglas GT's. These were belted bias-ply tires.

The radial tire uses a cord angle of ninety degrees, which means that the cords run directly across the tire from bead to bead. In addition, radial tires have belts, like the belted tires, under the tread. Because radials have flexible sidewalls, the tread is kept on the road surface longer during hard cornering, for better adhesion. Radial tires have less rolling resistance, resulting in better mileage; they also last much longer.

A good many of the radials available today are of the steel belted variety. I recommend staying away from them, as steel belts have a tendency to heat up, go out of round and cause tire failure under hard usage. Frequent bumps on the road will cause steel belts to deform. Unless the tire is specifically certified by the manufacturer as a performance tire, it would be wise to stay with a fiberglass, rayon or other type of belted radial.

Recently, some American manufacturers have started using European rating designations on their top-of-the-line performance tires. The highest rating, V, means that the tire is good for over 130 mph speeds.

Tire Speed Ratings
SR up to 112 mph
HR up to 130 mph
VR over 130 mph

You'll also note that tire size is measured differently today. Using the P-metric system, for example, an FR70x14 tire is now resized as a P205/70R14. (P stands for passenger tire; 205 is the section width of the tire in millimeters; 70 is the aspect ratio; R stands for radial; 14 stands for rim diameter in inches.) Also bear in mind that section width is not the same as tread width. For example, a B. F. Goodrich Radial T/A 70, P205/70R14, has a section width of 7.99 inches on a 5.5-inch-wide rim. Tread width measures six inches. Obviously, the larger the section width, the wider the tread. Also

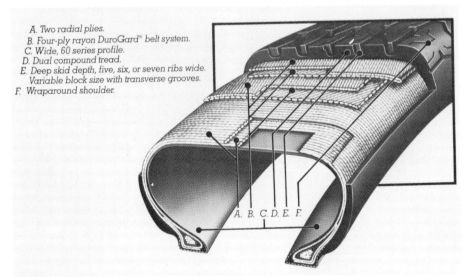

A. Two radial plies.
B. Four-ply rayon DuroGard® belt system.
C. Wide, 60 series profile.
D. Dual compound tread.
E. Deep skid depth, five, six, or seven ribs wide.
   Variable block size with transverse grooves.
F. Wraparound shoulder.

A. B. C. D. E. F.

This diagram shows how a high-performance radial, in this case B. F. Goodrich's Radial T/A, is constructed.

remember that section width varies approximately 0.2 inch for every 0.5 inch change in rim width.

Concerning high-speed driving, it is necessary to increase inflation pressure and it may be necessary to go to a larger tire because the original tire won't have sufficient strength. The chart shown below is taken from the *European Tyre and Rim Technical Organization Data Book.* According to the chart, for speeds up to 100 mph, standard inflation applies. For speeds over 130 mph, overloading may occur and tire upsizing may be needed.

For most street-performance Mustangs, it is unlikely that different tires will be required for high-speed driving, as the ninety-percent load capacity is at 137 mph. However, inflation should be increased. One thing to remember, though, is that the figures on the chart are *not* for original equipment or even most aftermarket tires, but rather for high-performance tires such as Goodyear's Eagle ST or B. F. Goodrich's Comp/TA.

After choosing the type of tire you'll put on your Mustang, the next factors to consider are diameter and height. If you are just going from a stock tire to a radial on the stock rim, you could probably increase tire tread by one or two sizes and not have any clearance problems. For example, a 1969 Mach I with a 428CJ-R came with F70x14 Polyglas tires. The equivalent radial size would be a P205/70R14. A P215/70R14 or a P225/70R14 would fit with no problems.

Problems arise when you decide to install larger-diameter rims as well as wider tires. Using the previous 1969 Mach I as an example, you can outfit it with 15x7 wheels, such as those that were stock on the Boss 302. You

VEHICLE TOP SPEED MPH	INFLATION PRESSURE INCREASE[1] PSI	LOAD CAPACITY[2] (% of maximum branded load on tire)
100	0	100
106	1.5	100
112	3.0	100
118	4.5	100
124	6.0	100
130	7.5	100
137	7.5	90
143	7.5	85
149	7.5	80
155	7.5	75
161	7.5	70
168	7.5	65
174	7.5	60
180	7.5	55
186	7.5	50

1-Do not exceed the maximum pressure branded on tire sidewall.
2-Tire upsizing may be necessary to achieve these reduced loads.

might as well pick a tire larger than the F60x15 original, such as a B. F. Goodrich P255/60VR15. This is approximately equivalent to a G or H60 size. This tire would probably fit the Mustang (with minor fender lip modification) but as it is taller, it would greatly affect that Mach I's axle ratio. The bigger the tire's diameter, the less acceleration, while a smaller-than-stock tire will improve acceleration.

The following formula will make it easy to find out what your effective axle ratio will be after changing from (for example) a stock F70x14 (P205/70R14) to a wider, taller P255/60VR15.

$$\frac{\text{New Tire Revs/Mile}}{\text{Original Tire Revs/Mile}} \times \text{Original Axle Ratio} = \text{Effective Axle Ratio}$$

For our Mach I example: $\dfrac{773}{825} \times 3.25 = 3.06$

The stock F70x14's on the 1969 428CJ Mach I are totally inadequate, yet despite such skinny tires, they are able to crank out low-14-, high-13-second quarter-mile times.

This 1967 Shelby has been updated with Goodyear Eagle NCT's, P255/60R15, equivalent to about a GR60x15. They are far superior than anything that was available in 1967.

Jacking the car up is not recommended and it is not the proper method to facilitate installing large tires on your Mustang.

Installing taller tires on the Mach I will now reduce the effective axle ratio from 3.25 to 3.06. This results in less acceleration but better highway mileage. To regain equivalent acceleration, the axle ratio must be changed.

If you decide to change the axle ratio to maintain stock acceleration, the following formula will tell you what axle ratio you will need.

$$\frac{\text{Original Tire Revs/Mile}}{\text{New Tire Revs/Mile}} \times \text{Original Axle Ratio} = \text{Equivalent Axle Ratio}$$

thus:

$$\frac{825}{773} \times 3.25 = 3.48$$

So, in order to duplicate stock acceleration, a 3.48 ratio is required. As Ford doesn't make a 3.48, the nearest size available, which is 3.50, should be installed.

Another point to consider with tires is aspect ratio. This is the tire casing height divided by the section width. Low-profile tires have a wider section and handle better because there is less side deflection during cornering, but they do lower the car, which may cause ground clearance problems on some Mustangs. Low-profile tires also give a much firmer ride. A good compromise on the street is a 60-series ratio.

Going to a lower aspect ratio may require taller rims in order to alleviate any ground clearance problems. That is why the SVO Mustang has sixteen-inch rims, to compensate for the 50-series Goodyears. For the average enthusiast, this can be an expensive proposition.

To summarize, get the widest radial that will fit your Mustang—highly recommended for earlier 1964-73 Mustangs that have bias and belted tires as stock.

WHEELS

Most Mustangs come stock from Ford with steel wheels. These do the job for a street vehicle, but for more cornering power, it is wise to invest in a wider

This 1969 Boss 429 has B. F. Goodrich Radial T/A's; GR50x15 in the front and LR50x15 in the back. In spite of large tire size, they don't hit the fenders.

set of wheels. A wider rim provides more support for the sidewalls so there is less deflection of the tire during cornering. Also, a wider tire can be installed. This means a higher limit of adhesion. As a rule of thumb, wheel width should equal tire section width, but with most Mustangs, this may have to be compromised because of insufficient clearance. Other advantages of using wider wheels, particularly aftermarket wheels, are that they increase wheel strength, improve brake cooling and lower unsprung weight.

Stock factory wheels are made of sheet steel. They are cheap and fairly light, yet are not strong enough to take the stress of road racing because they flex, particularly with wide tires. Aftermarket wheels, whether they are spoke or slot types, allow more air to circulate for brake cooling, which is advantageous. From a handling point of view, a lighter wheel is helpful because it reduces unsprung weight. Reducing unsprung weight enables the car to handle better on bumps; it can also make a difference when accelerating, as it takes less energy to rotate a lighter wheel assembly.

Most aftermarket wheels are made of aluminum and a weight saving of ten pounds per wheel is not uncommon. One point worth considering when buying new wheels is to make sure they have the SEMA (Specialty Equip-

This is what happens when you use wheels with negative offset. With proper care, you can install large tires without hitting the fenders.

This Boss 429 uses stronger, one-piece aftermarket aluminum wheels. These are American Racing's 200S.

ment Manufacturers Association) seal of approval. This means that the wheel has been designed to pass an endurance test so severe that many stock factory wheels cannot pass it. A one-piece-design wheel is stronger than a welded two-piece.

Before buying a set of wheels, check their offset and rear spacing and measure them to see how they compare with your stock wheels.

Rear spacing is easy to measure: It is the distance between the mounting surface of the wheel and the inboard edge of the rim. Measure the stock rims on your car to see how close the rim is to any part of the suspension so that you'll have a good idea of the maximum rear spacing that can be accommodated on your Mustang. Generally speaking, there is much more room in the rear and, with most older Mustangs, less room in the front.

Offset is the distance between the mounting surface of the wheel and the center of the wheel. Most stock Ford rims are zero offset, meaning the mounting surface of the wheel is exactly at the center. It is best to try to stay as close as possible to stock factory offset when purchasing a set of wheels. Positive offset occurs when the rim center is moved outward, which results in a wider track. Negative offset occurs when the center of the wheel is moved inward. This makes the track narrower, and results in the deep-dish look.

Wheels with positive offset can make the car corner faster because the wider track reduces weight transfer. However, positive offset puts extra strain on the wheel bearings, particularly during straight-line driving, while reducing loads during cornering. Small changes in offset don't affect bearing life enough to worry about but you should try to stay within the factory's specifications.

The key with wide wheels is to try to get the biggest wheels that will fit on your Mustang without going into excessive offset or resorting to expensive fender flares. Also, it is good to try to keep the same width rims front and rear.

SPRINGS

Here is another area the Mustang enthusiast may try to modify for better handling. However, it is one area that should be left alone and attention focused elsewhere. What you may think is a simple change can and does affect the car's handling in many different ways. I recommend changing springs only after radial tires, shocks and sway bars have been installed—

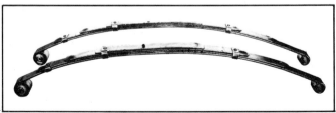

Most 1964-73 Mustangs can use stiffer rear springs. Photo courtesy Maier Racing Enterprises.

and only for the enthusiast who wants ultimate handling. Stiffer springs create a big compromise in ride quality.

Springs are designed to absorb bumps and other road irregularities. Soft springs give the best ride and the best traction on a rough road. The disadvantages of soft springs are poor cornering, lots of up and down movement, and diminished acceleration traction.

Stiffer springs enable the car to handle better, yet the ride will become firmer, and stiffer shocks will be necessary to control the springs. In many typical magazine articles you'll often find the suggestion that the 620-pound variety (or even 750 pounds) be installed in 1967-70 Mustangs. These may be fine on the track, but using them on the street will result in an intolerable ride and limited traction on any but the smoothest road surface. Stiffer springs also transfer shocks encountered on bumpy roads to the chassis and body, resulting in stress points and possible chassis cracking.

However, most Mustangs could use additional stiffening in the rear. Pre-1973 Mustangs are weak in this area and it is not uncommon to see Mustangs with a boat's nose-up attitude. Stiffening the rear springs will result in less understeer, too. The best way to go about this is to have the springs removed and replaced with stock new ones which are available from many Mustang parts dealers. A cheaper and equally effective answer is to install some leaf spring helpers. These do a good job. Air shocks can also be used, but you should avoid, if possible, the tendency to jack-up the rear.

SHOCKS

Most automobile manufacturers, including Ford, use the cheapest and softest shocks as standard equipment to provide the softest ride possible for normal driving. These just won't do for any sort of spirited driving.

Shocks control the up-and-down movement caused by the springs when the car hits a bump. Without shocks, the car's ride will be a series of bounces. The shock absorbs the energy generated when the wheel hits a bump and converts it to heat.

A typical factory shock absorber exerts its stiffening or dampening force mainly on the rebound stroke. When a wheel hits a bump, the shock offers small resistance. A stiff shock causes poor ride. The major portion of the shock's dampening action is exerted as the wheel is on its way back down to the road.

A helper spring, though, is a lot cheaper and just as effective. It clamps on the rear spring.

Shock stiffness must be matched to the car's springs. A heavier car with heavier springs requires a heavier-duty shock. This can be a problem for Mustangs. If you look at a shock manufacturer's catalog, often you'll find that, for example, one shock is designated for all 1967-70 Mustangs, whether they have have a six-cylinder engine or a heavy 390. Obviously the heavier the engine, the heavier the stock springs, so even aftermarket shocks are a compromise. From a handling point of view, it is necessary to invest in shock absorbers that can be adjusted to compensate for heavier springs or are designed exclusively for your application.

Many performance shock absorbers divide the dampening force closer to a 50-50 ratio, which results in a firmer ride, but improved handling.

Adjustable shocks are necessary if you want to fine tune your suspension. The usual method is to install the shocks at their softest setting and then measure how many times the car's body bounces when you push it down. Then increase the setting until the car just goes down and immediately comes back to rest—that should be in the ballpark.

There are many shocks available for Mustangs, and Koni shocks have always been a favorite. These are excellent-quality shocks but very expen-

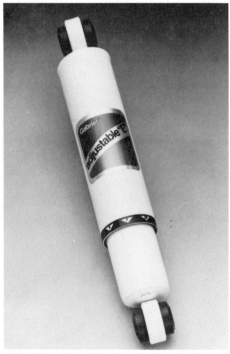

Koni shocks have been a favorite with Mustang owners for years, despite their high cost. These are the units available on the SVO Mustang and will fit other 1979 and later Mustangs. Photo courtesy Koni America, Inc.

Gabriel's adjustable shock absorbers are a low-cost alternative to more expensive adjustable shocks. Gabriel adjustables were optional on 1967 Mustangs and on 1975-78 Mustangs with the Competition Suspension. Photo Courtesy Maremont Corporation.

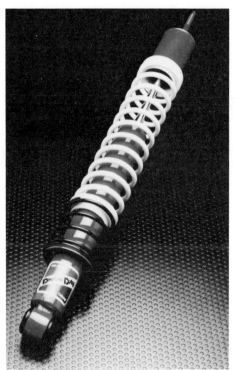

This type of heavy-duty shock uses two springs to compensate for additional load. Photo courtesy Maremont Corporation.

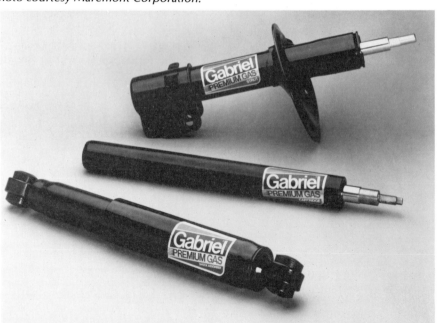

Gabriel's premium gas shocks use nitrogen gas to improve handling and control, and the gas provides a mild booster-spring effect. Photo courtesy Maremont Corporation.

sive. Gabriel makes a line of adjustable shocks that are adequate for street use and much more affordable.

A dual-purpose example is the rear air shocks. Their main purpose is to raise the ride height and provide stiffer springing action for cars that have to carry extra weight. Because they stiffen the rear springs and are also a good heavy-duty shock, they can improve the handling for many Mustangs. And, sometimes, a good air shock is all that is needed to clear rear tires that are slightly too large. However, too much air pressure will raise the car's height excessively and ride quality will deteriorate very rapidly.

Get the best shocks that you can afford for your Mustang. Poor shocks can spoil the handling of an otherwise well set up Mustang.

SWAY BARS

Adding a rear sway bar to your Mustang will improve its handling more than any other modification; it is also possibly the most cost effective change. This just can't be emphasized enough. The simple addition of a sway bar results in a phenomenal change (for the better) in your Mustang, especially on all the pre-1973 models. You need sway bars to be able to use the super and expensive tires. If you put a rear bar on a stock Mustang and super tires on another stock Mustang, the one with a rear bar would corner better because the Mustang with super tires wouldn't be able to take advantage of the big tires.

All Mustangs come with a front sway bar. For optimum handling these stock bars (no matter what size) are again a compromise, because they are not stiff enough to reduce body lean during high-speed cornering. They are designed for normal conservative driving, and the enthusiast will want more.

You can improve your Mustang's handling by installing a larger front bar. Most sources state that doing this will result in more understeer. This is usually true with cars that have similar front and rear suspension designs. On cars such as the Mustang, which have front independent suspension and

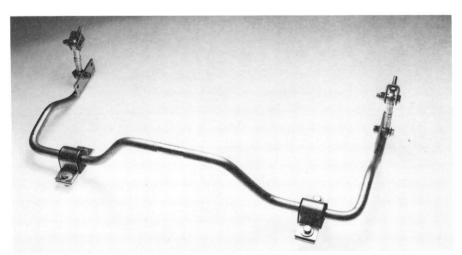

An adjustable front sway bar allows you to fine tune your suspension. Photo courtesy Quickor Engineering.

a solid rear axle, installing a larger front bar results in *less* understeer. The firmer front bar will prevent the wheels from leaning (camber change) during a turn, and this effect might be stronger than the extra weight transfer that occurs with a firmer bar.

However, considering the cost of a new front bar, and the slight improvement, it is much better to install a rear sway bar on your Mustang. The results are startling!

Sway bars are designed to twist when a car leans during a turn. When both wheels are pushed up, there is no loading on the sway bar. Any resistance or loading is exerted when only one wheel hits a bump or when the car is turning and leaning sharply in a turn. Thus a sway bar will stiffen a car's ride, but not nearly as much as firmer springs will. That is why stock springs are recommended. Stock springs with firm bars combine to provide good ride and flat cornering. This is what GM did with the Firebird/Camaro

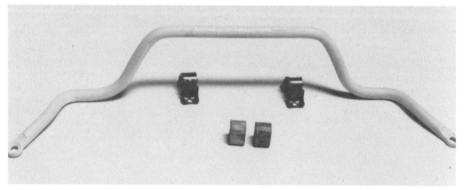

A rear sway bar will transform your Mustang into a handler. This is a hefty ⅞ inch rear bar for 1979-82 Mustangs. Photo courtesy DOBI.

Polyurethane bushings are advised for optimum handling. Photo courtesy Quickor Engineering.

during the seventies, while Mustang suspension development lagged.

Most stock Mustang front sway bars are mounted with rubber bushings and end links. Replacing these bushings on the chassis and end links with firm polyurethane bushings has a great effect on the sway bar and how the car handles. Solid bushings can make the stock bar act like, or have the same effect as, a 20-25 percent larger bar (rubber mounted). Such bushing kits are recommended as a low-cost solution to replacing your stock front bar.

Also make sure you get high-quality hardware, as sway bars place very heavy loads on mounting points. Photo courtesy Quickor Engineering.

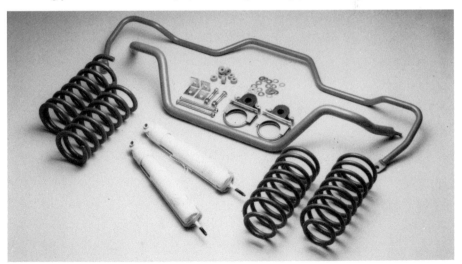

To completely transform your 1979 and later Mustang you have to change springs, sway bars and shocks. Photo courtesy DOBI.

Another consideration when selecting a bar is the material it is made from. Stock Ford sway bars are made from 4150H spring steel, a very good material. Some aftermarket suppliers, such as Stam-Bar Stabilizers, use even a better 5150H or 6150H spring steel. Avoid a sway bar made from 1018 cold-roll, mild steel. This material is easier and cheaper for manufacturing a bar, but it lacks the necessary spring qualities needed in a sway bar. Some manufacturers have tried to compensate by making the bar thicker, but this is not a good solution.

TRACTION BARS

These are devices used to limit leaf spring wind-up, wheel hop and the resulting loss of traction (1982 and later Mustangs use them too). These maladies are common with big-cubic-inch 1964-73 Mustangs. Less than ideal weight distribution, small tires and lots of low end torque can break the rear tires loose under hard acceleration. Traction bars are designed to limit wheel spin and hop; they were originally used on 1965-66 Shelby Mustangs. Traction bars work in the same way as the lower links used on coil-spring suspensions. They are attached to the axle housing and to the car's chassis. Cheaper units are also available that simply clamp on the spring near the axle and use a rubber snubber on the front part of the traction bar. Upon acceleration the snubber is raised against the spring, preventing spring wrap-up and resultant loss of traction. They are effective, but because they are mounted under the leaf spring, some ground clearance is lost.

Rather than resorting to traction bars with the hairy 428CJ Mustangs, Ford mounted the rear shocks in a new way. The shocks were staggered, meaning one shock, the left rear, was relocated behind the axle housing, while the other shock remained in the stock position in front of the housing.

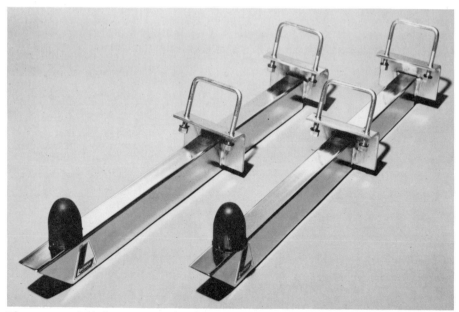

These are typical clamp on traction bars.

The shocks then prevented axle wind-up and wheel hop. Unfortunately, only four-speed Mustangs got this shock setup; however, it is standard equipment on all 1974-78 Mustang II's.

FRONT BAR		REAR BAR	
5/8	100%	1/2	100%
3/4	160%	5/8	167%
7/8	200%	11/16	179%
15/16	210%	3/4	212%
1	226%	7/8	222%
1-1/8	244%	15/16	228%

These two charts show the difference or increase in torsional stiffness as sway bar size increases.

BALLAST

A good way to improve weight distribution on your Mustang is to relocate the battery to the trunk. The early 1965 Shelby GT350 and the 1969-70 Boss 429 Mustang had the battery in the trunk. This was done to improve weight distribution, especially on the big-block 429. A typical battery weighs about thirty pounds. Moving the battery to the trunk results in about a one-percent rear weight shift which provides a noticeable effect on handling. It should be mounted on the right rear part of the trunk to aid traction. Direct Connection, the Chrysler performance parts subsidiary, markets a simple kit that includes brackets, cable and hardware; or you can just as easily make your own, using about twenty-five feet of welding cable, battery terminal ends, a battery tray and a marine-type battery case. You may also want to factor in the weight of the gas tank. A full tank of gas weighs close to 100 pounds, and this can make a big difference in weight distribution.

One other method of reducing front weight (and thereby improving

This type of traction bar was used on 1966 Shelby Mustangs, and fits other Mustangs as well.

handling) is to switch to a fiberglass hood. These weigh much less than stock steel hoods and a weight savings of fifty pounds is possible. All Shelby Mustangs have fiberglass hoods.

The substitution of the stock cast iron intake manifold, particularly on the 390/428 engines, with an aluminum unit will have a positive effect on handling. The stock manifold is a big hunk of iron weighing 100 pounds. An aluminum manifold can save up to 60-65 pounds, depending on manufacturer.

SUSPENSION MODIFICATIONS

Generally speaking, don't. Relocation of suspension components requires a high degree of knowledge and skill. While these sorts of modification, such as those in the Boss 302 handling guide, are designed to provide

Relocating the battery to the trunk helps weight distribution.

Lowering the upper control A-arm on 1964-70 Mustangs is a labor-only operation that improves handling.

superior handling on the racetrack, they are too much of a compromise for a street Mustang. It is best to leave the suspension in stock configuration.

However, on 1965-70 Mustangs, there is a relatively simple modification that has become pretty much standard fare. This involves lowering the upper control arms. This modification is designed to increase cornering power by about eight percent.

A template is provided in this book's appendix and it is basically a labor-only modification (no additional parts needed). The result is better cornering and a lower front end for that racer look.

The only other modification that is recommended, and this applies to 1965-70 Mustangs, is to install the stronger export-shock-to-firewall brace. This extra triangulation adds rigidity to the Mustang structure and thus improves handling. A Monte Carlo bar, which links the shock towers together, is also beneficial.

Using a stronger export brace on your 1964-70 Mustang effectively stiffens the front end. Stock brace is a two-piece unit that bends easily.

This Mustang has the export brace plus a specially made Monte Carlo bar to clear the dual-quad air cleaner.

Suspension development continues with the 1985 Mustang GT. The TRX wheels are replaced with much superior Goodyear P225/60VRx15 Gatorback tires on 15x7 inch rims. Additionally, the Mustang's chassis is stiffened and reinforced, which contributes to better handling.

Spoilers appeared first on 1969 Boss 302 Mustangs; they are effective at high speeds.

AERODYNAMICS

There are devices designed to combat aerodynamic lift of the front end and to increase downward rear pressure to improve traction. You have to be moving pretty fast (more than 80 mph) for spoilers, wings, air dams and so on to have any effect. However, a front spoiler or air dam can be effective in increasing highway mileage at legal speeds. Moreover, spoilers improve the car's image which is probably the biggest reason most enthusiasts opt for them.

Ford introduced a front spoiler, a rear wing and a spoilered tail on the 1969 Boss 302 Mustang. They were basically for image, although they were used on the Boss 302 Trans-Am race cars. Ford continued the spoilers and wings on the later 1971-73 Mustangs and these are still popular add-ons.

For the record, the Shelby Mustangs were the first to incorporate aerodynamics into Mustang styling beginning in 1967. A large, tall spoiler was incorporated in the trunk lid. Earlier Shelby Mustangs had available a special front apron designed to duct more air to the radiator and front brakes, and a special rear window designed to increase top speed on a race Shelby.

Aerodynamics, at least from the styling point of view, emerged again in 1976, with the Cobra II. These are probably effective yet, again, Ford made no mention of any sort of improvement attributed to the front and rear spoilers. The ultimate aerodynamic package for the Mustang II was the King

Spoilers continued to be popular on 1971-73 Mustangs such as this 1971 Boss 351. Randy Ream photo.

The 1967 Shelby Mustang was the first to have an integral rear spoiler.

Cobra, which incorporated a front air dam.

The newer 1979 and later Mustangs use air dams, spoilers and the like, primarily for image. The latest design, from the aftermarket, introduces side skirts to simulate a "ground effects" race car. Kamei makes a very striking package for the Mustang.

BRAKES

If you plan to drive fast, make sure that your Mustang will also stop

Another interesting Shelby innovation was this modified rear window which increased top speed by at least 5 mph. Alan Bolte photo.

The effect may be questionable at legal speeds, but the X-1 package for the 1979 and later Mustangs made by Kamei is certainly impressive. Photo courtesy Kamei USA Auto Extras.

quickly. This means, at a minimum, front disc brakes. If you have drums all around, and you want a good-handling Mustang, you have to install disc brakes in the front. This is not a difficult operation, as the parts are easily available. Fortunately, all 1974 and later Mustangs have front disc brakes.

Here are some common sense suggestions that are helpful. First, make sure your discs and drums are balanced and that both are machined smooth. Use premium pads and shoes. A good choice for a dual-purpose vehicle would be semimetallic pads, which last longer and provide better braking action.

Another useful modification would be to install steel braided hoses in place of the stock rubber brake hoses at the wheels. When the brakes are

Good-quality brake pads and shoes are necessary for safe braking. Photo courtesy DOBI.

used hard, hydraulic pressure causes the stock hoses to expand, which creates a softer pedal and requires more pumping. These hoses can be obtained from Earl's Supply Company or from other sources listed in the back of this book.

Switching to silicone-base brake fluid is also a good idea. Silicone fluid does not absorb moisture and thus can maintain a high boiling point. Heat deteriorates regular brake fluid, which then picks up moisture, resulting in a mushy brake pedal during hard use. Boiling fluid is a major cause of brake problems under severe use, particularly with disc brakes.

At this point I must caution you not to mix regular and silicone fluids together. The old brake fluid must first be flushed out and the whole system then flushed with alcohol to purge it of any old fluid and moisture. Then your system is ready for silicone-base fluid.

By far the best brake modification is to install rear disc brakes on your Mustang. The stock drums, which work fine in normal use, cannot dissipate the heat quickly enough in severe use, and the brakes fade. Installing rear disc brakes will overcome this problem, and your Mustang will stop faster.

This modification has become quite popular for 1965-73 Mustangs with eight- or nine-inch rears. There are various methods to install four-wheel disc brakes. One method to consider is outlined in the Boss 302 handling book, where 1969 Lincoln front discs are adapted and used in the rear. Although effective, this is expensive, parts are hard to locate and there is no emergency brake provision. Another way is to use a complete rear from a late Lincoln Versailles which has rear discs. This is a tough item to find in the junkyard and, when found, can be costly. You can also use a kit to adapt the

The holes in this Mustang rotor have been redrilled to fit the larger rear axle studs. You can either drill new holes, as on this rotor, or redrill existing holes. Photo courtesy Total Performance Magazine.

Lincoln brakes to your Mustang but this, again, has the drawback of high cost.

The easiest and probably most economical way to install rear discs is to use the system used by Shelby representative and owner Pete Buompane. His conversion is designed to work with 1967 and later Mustangs that already have front disc brakes. Listed below are the parts necessary:

1. Two 1965-67 Mustang front rotors
2. Two 1979 Pontiac Trans Am rear disc backing plates, part numbers 10004494 and 10004495
3. Two Pontiac Trans Am rear disc brake calipers, part numbers 18005294 and 18005295
4. One Mustang left-hand parking brake cable—driver's side
5. One 1973 Montego right-hand parking brake cable part number D20Z-2A635-A
6. One 1973 Montego center cable, part number D20Z-2A815-A
7. One M-2328-A Ford Motorsport brake proportioning valve

The only machining required is to enlarge the existing holes in the rotors so that the rear axle studs fit through the rotors. Then you must have the outside diameter of the axle flange turned down so that it will fit inside the rotor hub.

Begin by removing the stock brake drums, backing plates, shoes and so on, and the rear axles. Then mount the Pontiac caliper on the new backing plate. Compare this assembly to the axle housing flange. The hole in the backing plate must be centered with the hole in the axle housing. Position the backing plate so that the caliper is at the nine o'clock position (both left

Here the caliper is mounted on the backing plate and rear axle is installed. Outside diameter of axle flange has been turned down to fit the Mustang front rotor. Photo courtesy Total Performance Magazine.

and right rear). Once the backing plate hole is centered with the axle center hole, scribe the pattern of the four axle housing holes on the backing plate. Then drill the new holes in the backing plate. The only other operation needed is to slightly open up the center hole of the backing plate so that the axle bearing can slip through it.

Final assembly starts with slipping the axle through the backing plate and then bolting the backing plate and axle plate onto the axle housing. Then install the rotors, calipers, brake lines and emergency cable lines.

Finally, install the brake proportioning valve in the rear brake line and, after some experimentation, adjust the valve for optimum brake performance. In this case, the front wheels should lock up slightly before the rear wheels do.

In addition, the stock master cylinder will have to be modified to divide the brake pressure equally front and rear. This is done by removing the black plastic residual valve and spring located in the rear pressure plate of the

Adjustable proportioning valve is necessary for this conversion. Photo courtesy Maier Racing Enterprises.

It is a clean installation and there are no extra brackets and hardware to get in the way. Note rear sway bar and traction bars used on this Shelby. Photo courtesy Total Performance Magazine.

master cylinder. First remove the line, remove the brass orifice in the port, remove the black residual valve and spring, then reinstall the brass orifice and brake line.

You'll note the use of the Montego brake cable for the passenger-side

This is what a completed conversion looks like—a factory installation. Note that passenger-side caliper faces to the rear. Photo courtesy Total Performance Magazine.

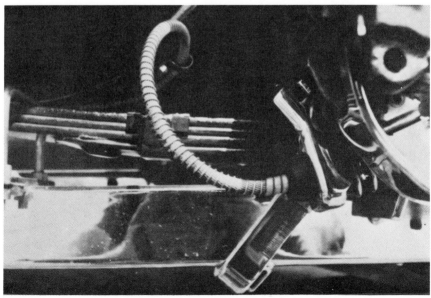

Shown here is the rear emergency brake hookup, one of the good features of this conversion. Photo courtesy Total Performance Magazine.

hookup. This cable is about eighteen inches longer than the Mustang passenger-side cable and is needed to reach around the back of the caliper mounted on the passenger side. The driver's side can use the stock cable.

The big advantage, besides cost, with this system is the retention of emergency brakes. Although there is a difference in thickness between Pontiac and Ford rotors, this is no problem because the calipers are a full floating design.

Although the combination of Ford and Pontiac parts may seem a little odd, the parts are compatible and this is an easy way to dramatically improve your Mustang's braking.

ALIGNMENT

The alignment angles of the front suspension exert an influence on the car's steering ease, steering stability, ride quality and tire wear. This can be a complex subject because these angles vary as the suspension does its job and the body moves up and down in relation to the wheels. The load in a car and its speed may also cause these angles to change. In addition, they are affected by changes in the car's attitude caused by acceleration, braking and the type of road surface and cornering forces.

Camber is the amount (in degrees) that the front wheels tilt in or out at the top when viewed from the front of the car. When the top of the wheel leans inward, camber is negative. It is best to try for zero camber when aligning the front wheels. A little negative camber will help cornering, from 0-½ degree, but any more than this will cause uneven tire wear. With zero camber, the full width of the tire's tread makes contact with the road.

Caster refers to the angle made by a line between the upper and lower steering pivots (ball joints) and a vertical reference line. The angle is positive when this line tilts backward (when the upper ball joint is behind the lower ball joint). It is negative when this line tilts forward (upper ball joint is in front of the lower). Caster is important as it aids directional stability, increases steering returnability and reduces steering effort. Positive caster tends to keep the wheels pointed straight ahead and reduces any tendency for the car to wander at high speed. Too much positive caster increases steering effort. A good maximum for a street-driven Mustang is two degrees positive. Caster can also be affected by weak or sagging springs. Front spring sag decreases positive caster, while rear spring sag increases positive caster.

Toe is usually set "in," measured in inches. Toe-in increases high-speed stability and takes the slack out of the suspension as the car moves from rest. Incorrect toe greatly affects tire wear. Stay within factory specifications, which for Mustangs up to 1978 is ⅛ inch toe-in.

Because of the MacPherson strut front-suspension design used on 1979 and later Mustangs, caster and camber angles are preset at the factory and cannot be changed. Toe, however, is adjustable. Of course, by using specially fabricated camber plates, camber can be changed, but this is usually done only on race Mustangs.

CHAPTER 14

1964-1966 HANDLING RECOMMENDATIONS

The hottest and best-performing street Mustang made in this group is the Shelby GT350. Although this is not a true factory Mustang, the modifications made by Carroll Shelby are useful and applicable to other Mustangs. These early Shelby Mustangs are about as close to a racer as an enthusiast's car can be and still be considered a street car. Shelby modified the Mustangs exactly as the typical Mustang enthusiast would and then sold them to the public. A strong engine was not the only part of the package; the chassis, driveline, suspension and brakes were also modified so the car would handle well. By combining some of the features of the GT350 along with a few other recommendations you will have a 1964½-66 Mustang that is both safer and much more fun to drive!

The early Shelby used very, very stiff springs. Unless you like a hard, uncomfortable ride, I would recommend retaining your stock front springs and then using either new springs in the rear or helper springs to stiffen the rear a bit. Mustang rear springs have a reputation for being marginal and can always use some firming up.

It is also not necessary to use the Shelby's one-inch front sway bar. The original bar on all stock Mustangs was a small ⅝ inch bar. The GT Mustangs and all those with the 271 hp High Performance 289 got a 13/16 inch bar. The first steps in either case are to install a ⅝ inch rear bar and to use polyurethane bushing on the front bar. Your Mustang will still understeer, but much, much less. For even less understeer, use an 11/16 inch rear bar.

Other performance Mustangs, such as the Shelby, should start with an

125

11/16 inch rear bar and the polyurethane front bushings. A larger bar than 11/16 in the rear may be too much for a street-driven Mustang with street tires. Some experimentation is required to get the best combination.

The ultimate in sway bars, for best performance, is an adjustable sway bar. With an adjustable bar you can adjust for understeer and camber change and still maintain a good ride.

Regarding tires, six-cylinder and some V-8 Mustangs of 1964½-65 vintage are at a serious disadvantage. These Mustangs are equipped with four-bolt thirteen-inch wheels. Changing to a more reasonable five-bolt fourteen-inch wheel (standard with V-8's) is an expensive proposition. However, if you are stuck with small wheels, try to get the largest radial in a 70-series profile that will fit on your wheels. Other 1965 models, along with the 1966, can use a 205/70R14, which is equivalent to an FR70x14, one size larger than stock. This size of tire will not cause any fender clearance problems and is a worthwhile addition if you want to maintain stock Mustang appearance. The biggest tire that you can probably install on the stock rims (depending on manufacturer) would be a P215/70R14 or a P225/70R14. Going to a 60-series tire would yield better handling, but since a 60-series tire is wider, it is wise to stay with a 70-series size to avoid any problems. Going to a larger, wider tire will probably require some flattening of the inner fender lips to gain clearance.

Early Shelby Mustangs came with 15x6 inch rims and 7.75x15 Goodyear Blue Dot tires. These tires, great in their day, have been eclipsed by radial tires. As with other Mustangs, wider lower-profile radials can be installed on wider rims. The maximum workable size is 15x7 inches, and this depends on the wheel's offset. Tire size, again, depends on the make of tire and the

Your best bet is to emulate the good handling qualities built into the GT350 Mustang. Rick Kopec photo.

extent to which you want to modify your fenders. Some owners have managed to fit rather large tires on their Shelby with minor fender modifications, but even so, it seems that an occasional rub occurs. For a trouble-free installation, stay with a P215/70R15 or a P215/60R15 size.

I am not making any specific recommendations regarding tire make. There are several brands that offer outstanding performance and each major manufacturer has an excellent top-of-the-line performance tire.

Mustangs with manual steering can benefit from the installation of a quick-steering kit which replaces the stock Pitman and idler arms. This modification was standard equipment on the Shelby Mustang. It offers better steering response at high speeds.

You can also lower your Mustang's front suspension upper A-arms for improved handling. Just use the template provided in this book's appendix.

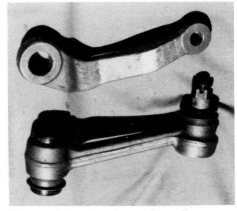

The quick-steering kit works well on non-Shelby Mustangs too.

A modern radial tire is mandatory for good handling. This GT350 has P215/70R14 Goodyear Eagle ST's on 14x6 Magnum rims. These provide excellent traction with no interference.

This Shelby is using a stronger aftermarket aluminum wheel with old-style Polyglas tires.

Heavy-duty shocks are very desirable, and it is preferable to install adjustable shocks. Koni shocks were standard equipment on the 1965 Shelby, but are very expensive. However, they are rebuildable and will usually last the life of your Mustang.

Finally, installing an export brace will effectively add rigidity to the front body structure.

These modifications will result in a Mustang that will handle better and be much more satisfying to drive!

The export brace and Monte Carlo bar are helpful in adding rigidity to the Mustang's front end.

The Shelby racing apron improves cooling to the radiator and has ducting to cool the brakes. It is more of an image modification for street Mustangs.

This Mustang convertible has been modified with fender flares, Shelby apron and front spoiler. Not easily visible are the rocker panel skirts.

This Mustang fastback features less radical modifications. Note low-profile, wide tires.

CHAPTER 15

1967-1970 HANDLING RECOMMENDATIONS

In 1967 Ford gave the Mustang a wider track, revised front suspension and strengthened the car to cope with the installation of big-block engines, which resulted in a better riding and handling Mustang. Still, as with earlier Mustangs, there was too much understeer built in and too much roll or leaning during cornering.

Modifications on these Mustangs follow the same pattern as for earlier Mustangs: Leave the front springs alone and firm up the rear springs. Installation of the 200-pound-per-inch rear springs is worthwhile; at the very least, use helper springs. When Ford put the big 390 in the Mustang, it put in heavier front springs but left the rear springs alone.

In conjunction with firmer springs, use the best shocks that you can afford. If you have adjustable shocks on a big-block Mustang, set the front shocks to full firm and the rears to a medium setting.

The 1967-70 Mustangs have a much greater choice of stock front sway bars: 5/8, 11/16, 3/4, 7/8 and 15/16 inch. The largest bar was used on most of the performance Mustangs, whether they had a small- or big-block engine. In 1970, Ford finally saw fit to install a rear sway bar on the Mach I and Boss 302/429 models. These were either a ½ inch bar on the 351 Mach I and Boss 302 or a ⅝ inch bar on the big-block 428 and 429. The first Mustang to receive a rear sway bar was the limited production 1969 Boss 429, which had a ¾ inch bar.

Whatever front bar your Mustang has, install a rear bar first. Although you could use the factory ⅝ rear, it is better to install an aftermarket bar because it has longer arms and, therefore, provides more antiroll control than the stock Ford bar. The ½ inch Ford bar is not very useful and is not

Typical front suspension design of all 1964½-73 Mustangs. This is of a 1970 Boss 302. Front disc brakes are necessary for good handling.

Beginning with most 1969 Performance Mustangs, the front shock towers received extra strengthening to accommodate the stress exerted by the new F60 tires. If your Mustang has stock-type towers (left), it is suggested that they be strengthened accordingly.

recommended. For more serious handling, you can install a larger 11/16 rear bar in conjunction with firmer front bushings. All big-block Mustangs should have the 15/16 inch front bar, preferably with polyurethane mounts in conjunction with an 11/16 or even a ¾ inch rear bar. One manufacturer, Addco Industries, makes a ⅞ inch rear bar, but this is only recommended for autocrossing or racing.

Boss 302's would have benefited from a rear bar in 1969, and a ⅝ inch bar is a good choice today. Front bar on these Mustangs should also be increased to 15/16 inch.

Lowering the front suspension is also beneficial. The template provided in the appendix should ease this operation.

You can gain additional front end rigidity by using the same export brace that fits the 1965-66 Shelby Mustang along with a Monte Carlo bar. All 1967-70 Shelby Mustangs and Boss 429 Mustangs came with an export brace as standard equipment.

Best-handling big-block Mustang is the 1969-70 Boss 429. It has lowered front suspension along with wider track, very firm springs and it was the first Mustang with a rear sway bar, ¾ inch in 1969 and ⅝ inch in 1970. This is a 1970. Dane Miller photo.

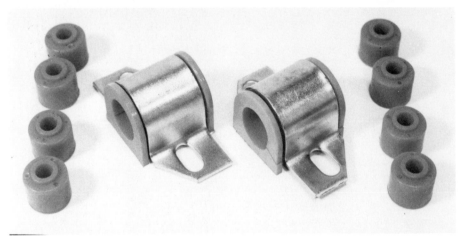

Using polyurethane bushings and end link bushings allows you to effectively firm up your Mustang's front bar.

The 1967-70 Mustangs are much heavier, especially those with big-block engines. It is important to retain power steering and power brakes if your Mustang already has them. Converting to manual steering for street use is not recommended and converting to power steering is beneficial to Mustangs with larger, wider tires. In addition, the power-steering box provides a 16:1 ratio for faster turning.

Nineteen sixty-seven and later Mustangs have larger wheel openings and thus can accommodate larger, wider tires much more easily than 1964-66's. Six-cylinder Mustangs are at a disadvantage because they were originally equipped with four-bolt lugs until 1970, although they did have

1967-70 Mustangs have larger wheelhouses allowing for larger than stock tires and wheels.

fourteen-inch wheels. Most other Mustangs came with 14x6 inch rims, even the powerful 428CJ-equipped Mustangs (14x7 in 1970). These clearly could use more tire.

A P205/70R14 radial is a good choice for a stock replacement size. A 60-series radial is better for handling and there are more sizes to choose from for the Mustangs. About the widest rim that can be fitted on 1967-70 Mustangs is seven inches, provided that stock offset and rear spacing is

This shot shows rear disc brake, narrow leaf springs, override traction bars, disconnected sway bar. Dale Sale photo.

The Trans-Am Mustang has heavy-duty tie rods and drag link to improve bump steer. Lower control arms have been reinforced and sway bar is attached on solid mounts. Note large, 13 quart oil pan. Custom-made headers are designed for maximum lowering of car. Dale Sale photo.

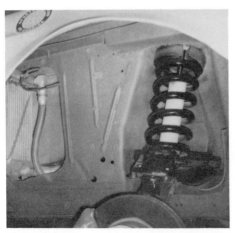

Shot of front suspension shows Boss 429 upper control arm. Note torque box up by top of spring. This is for shock tower reinforcement. On the left is the engine oil cooler. Dale Sale photo.

This shot shows further rear suspension modifications. Line attached to axle housing goes to small oil cooler mounted in front of rear axle. Dale Sale photo.

maintained. This applies to both fourteen- and fifteen-inch-diameter front wheels. Larger wheels can be fitted in the rear provided the offset is correct. It can be difficult finding wheels larger than seven-inches with the offset necessary to keep the wheel under the rear fenders; most aftermarket wheels have more negative offset as they get wider, for that deep-dish look.

If it is within your budget, try to switch to a 15x7 inch wheel. This size was standard equipment on all 1967-70 Shelby Mustangs and all the Boss series Mustangs. You can fit very wide tires on these rims and the only modification required is to pound in the inner lips of the fenders. All 1969-70 Boss Mustangs had this modification as standard.

You'll note that photographs are included of the suspension modifications made on the 1969-70 Trans-Am Mustangs. As you can see, the changes made aren't very radical and, at first glance, the suspension looks stock.

A high point in Mustang handling was reached with the 1970 Trans-Am Series Mustang. Appearancewise it's hard to tell that it is actually an all-out race car. Dale Sale photo.

CHAPTER 16

1971-1973 HANDLING RECOMMENDATIONS

These are the last first-generation Mustangs; they're also the biggest and heaviest. Ford did improve the suspension of these big Mustangs, although the same basic design was used. Competition Suspension-equipped Mustangs got variable ratio steering (made by GM), which improved steering and steering response. A rear sway bar was part of the Competition Suspension, and the front of the car was stronger than previous Mustangs so that front end rigidity was not as much of a problem. However, these Mustangs still had lots of understeer built into the suspension, and they were not known as excellent handlers as they came from the factory. True, they feel better than other Mustangs when driven moderately but when driven hard they exhibit less than optimum handling characteristics.

Ford did not modify the suspension during this Mustang's production run. At the same time, less interest has been shown in the aftermarket to develop equipment for workable suspension modifications. Basically, if you own a 1971-73 Mustang, there is little that you can do, but even so, this last big Mustang can be made to handle better.

Regarding springs, the advice given on earlier Mustangs applies. Try to firm up the rear a bit. It seems that all 1971-73 Mustangs exhibit a nose-up attitude which detracts from good handling. Good firm shocks can also help.

Front sway bar size is either ⅞ or ¾ inch, depending on the Mustang's engine. Competition Suspension-equipped cars came with a ½ inch rear bar, while the Boss 351 and 429 Mach I's and Mustangs got a slightly larger ⅝ inch rear bar. These bars are inadequate and should be replaced.

Focusing on the rear, at a minimum use a ¾ inch rear bar. Addco also has a ⅞ inch rear bar, but this is not recommended for the street. In the front, use the one-inch bar that is available from several sources. (There is also a

An adjustable rear sway bar is very useful in modifying the biggest Mustang's handling characteristics. Photo courtesy Maier Racing Enterprises.

1971-73 Mach I's came with front and rear bars. Only the 429 and Boss 351 had the larger ⅝ rear bar. Wheelhouses allow for large tires. This is a 1971 429CJ. Bobby Spedale photo.

1973 Mach I's were available with one-piece aluminum wheels. Rim size, unfortunately, was limited to 14 inches. Brent Galloway photo.

larger 1⅛ inch bar available from Quickor Engineering.) Again, mounting the bars with polyurethane bushings will enhance the effect on your Mustang.

There is no problem with fitting wider tires to these Mustangs. The Boss 351 came with 15x7 inch wheels which were optional on other 1971-72 Mustangs. Recommendations are the same as those for 1967-70 Mustangs.

The enterprising owner of this model fabricated a front air dam and side skirts for his Mustang.

CHAPTER 17

1974-1978 HANDLING RECOMMENDATIONS

The second-generation Mustang was quite a departure from the original. Performance was an important consideration in the first Mustang, but with the Mustang II, fuel economy, comfort and a smooth ride were primary concerns. Performance didn't appear again until 1975, when a low-horsepower 302 was introduced, in response to pressure from performance-minded enthusiasts.

The front suspension was redesigned, with the coil spring mounted on the lower control arm and the whole front suspension was mounted on an isolated subframe designed to reduce road noise and rough ride. The rear suspension remained the same, but through the liberal use of rubber, it was made quieter and more comfortable. The rear shocks, though, were staggered like those on earlier performance Mustangs. Front disc brakes and a front sway bar were standard equipment on all models. Mustangs with the Rallye or Competition Suspension also got a rear sway bar. The liberal use of rubber on the Mustang's suspension and chassis tended to make the car less responsive during hard cornering, and it lacked a solid feel.

Standard wheels were thirteen inches in diameter as were the radial tires. Standard tire size was BR78x13, rather small. Optional five-inch wheels were available in various configurations fitted with CR70x13 tires. These were not quite enough for a 302-equipped Mustang II.

You can outfit your Mustang II with larger tires, as there are many brands available for thirteen-inch rims. Though it is possible to fit 50-series tires, some ground clearance would be lost. It would be better to install fourteen-inch rims with a 50- or 60-series tires to maintain sufficient ground clearance. As with other Mustangs, outfitting wider tires may require pounding out the inner fender lips for clearance. However, fourteen-inch wheels and tires do a lot to improve the performance image of Mustang II's.

One nice point with Competition Suspension Mustangs is that they came with adjustable shocks. A full firm setting is required with the 302 engine.

Stock sway bars on the Mustang II consisted of a 13/16 inch front sway bar on four- and six-cylinder cars while the 302's got a 15/16 inch front bar. The Competition Suspension package used a one-inch front bar and an 11/16 inch rear bar with four- and six-cylinder Mustangs, while the heavier 302 got a ¾ inch bar.

To reduce understeer, the best thing you can do is to install a rear sway bar in conjunction with polyurethane bushings in the front. Addco Industries has a ⅞ inch rear bar, as does Quickor Engineering. In addition, Quickor also offers a smaller ¾ inch rear bar. However, both these bars are recommended only with 302-equipped Mustang II's that have a limited slip rear and wider than stock tires, otherwise they introduce a lot of oversteer into the chassis.

In the front, a one-inch bar is recommended, and you can either use a Ford bar or one from Addco or Quickor. Quickor also sells a large 1⅛ inch front bar for serious use.

Over the years, the Mustang II has been pooh-poohed as not being a performance car, yet with simple, logical modifications it can be made to perform, like any other Mustang.

Front suspension was redesigned on the Mustang II. Spring is mounted under upper control arm. Disc brakes are standard equipment on all Mustang II's.

The wheelwells on these Mustangs can accommodate larger tires with no problem. Ed Gribble photo.

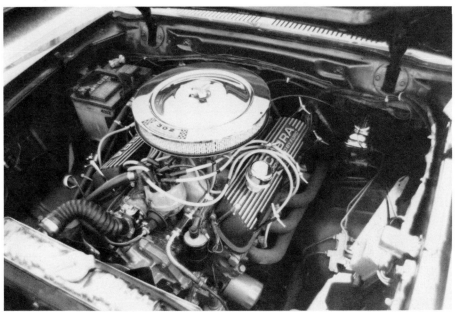

With a modified 302 the Mustang II becomes a serious street contender.

High point for the 1974-78 Mustangs is the King Cobra. Dale Rabe photo.

CHAPTER 18

1979-1985 HANDLING RECOMMENDATIONS

The 1979 and later Mustangs bear little resemblance to earlier models. These cars were totally redesigned to provide more practical transportation and be more competitive with the imports. Ford tried to placate enthusiasts this time around by introducing performance engines and suspension packages. The newer Mustangs *are* better handlers than most of the 1964-78 vintage stock Mustangs. However, in order for the newer Mustangs to compete with the newest Camaro/Trans Am, it is up to the enthusiast to go the extra mile, as even the most performance-oriented stock Mustangs, and that includes the SVO, need some attention and modification to be truly outstanding performers.

The front suspension was totally redesigned for the 1979 Mustang. In fact, it was borrowed from the Fairmont. This is a strut-type suspension that uses a strut to replace the conventional upper A-arm. The coil spring is located on the lower arm and on the chassis. This type of suspension is found on most imported cars and has the advantage of being cheaper to manufacture. The rear suspension utilizes coil springs with four bar links to locate the rear axle with conventional rear shocks. Liberal use of rubber bushings is intended to produce a comfortable ride.

All Mustangs have a front sway bar as standard equipment. No rear bar is available with the base suspension; however, a rear bar is included with the optional 302 and is also part of the handling suspension. Rear bar sizes have varied through the years ranging from 0.50 to 0.67 inch. The larger size was first available in 1983, in an effort to improve the Mustang's handling.

A good deal of effort went into designing the top optional suspension for the Mustang: the TRX system. Different shock valving and spring rates, and larger sway bars (1.12 inches in the front and with the rear bar varying in size as mentioned before) are part of the package. However, the improved handling is mostly due to the Michelin TRX tires, which use a specially

The best-handling factory Mustang in this generation is the SVO Mustang.

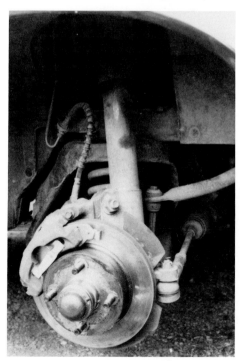

Front suspension uses a MacPherson strut. Disc brakes are standard equipment.

Rear suspension uses coil springs. SVO Mustang has rear disc brakes.

143

designed aluminum wheel measuring 15.4x5.9 inches. Tire size was 190/65R. In 1983 these tires were upgraded with a larger 220 size, along with a different rubber compound to improve handling and traction. The TRX option, although expensive, has proven to be very popular.

The base Mustang in 1979 came with small 13x5 inch wheels, which have since been dropped. The optional handling suspension uses 14x5.5 inch wheels and the TRX system continued with the special aluminum rims until 1984. The 1984 SVO, which used 50-series tires (Goodyear NCT radials, 225/50VR16) on 16x7 inch alloy rims. Sixteen-inch rims are used to compensate for the very low profile Goodyear radials. These are, by the way,

Part of the credit goes to the 16x7 inch rims with Goodyear 225/50VR15 tires on the SVO. These 50-series tires are good to speeds over 130 mph.

The TRX suspension package has been very popular and is recognizable by these unique wheels.

rated V, good for over 130 mph.

Steering on the Mustang is rack and pinion with power assist. Front brakes are discs on all Mustangs, and the SVO has an upgraded system utilizing discs on all four wheels.

Speaking of the SVO, its front suspension is further refined from other production Mustangs, using different spring and shock rates along with a different lower control arm from the Lincoln. The rear suspension, again, is refined with a different sway bar and the SVO uses a unique set of hydraulic dampeners to replace the traction bars that performance Mustangs have used since 1982. These resemble shock absorbers mounted horizontally between the ends of the rear axle and the chassis.

There is no doubt that Ford has done a creditable job in upgrading the Mustang's handling characteristics, especially with the TRX suspension. Unfortunately, from an enthusiast's point of view, the Mustang still understeers too much and leans too much during cornering. In addition, during hard cornering and accelerating out of a corner, any road surface irregularity will cause the rear wheels to break loose, resulting in severe wheel hop. This is the result of compliant rear suspension bushings. Even the SVO suffers from this malady. The TRX tires aren't wide enough for the 302 power, especially for a modified 302.

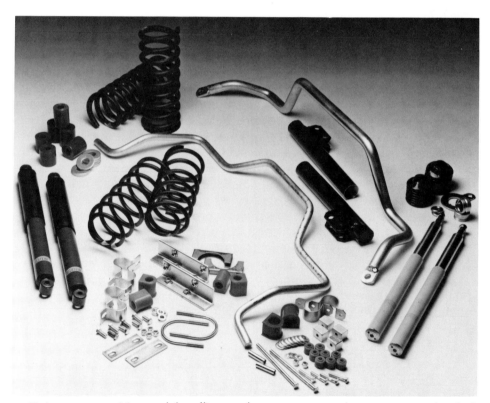

To improve your Mustang's handling you have to go to a total systems approach, which means replacement of the factory springs, shocks and sway bars. Photo courtesy Quickor Engineering.

More than for any other Mustang, the cure to all these problems seems to be a total systems approach, meaning replacement of the stock springs (to lower the center of gravity), sway bars, shocks/struts and rear axle bushings, and upgrading the stock wheels and tires. There are different ways of doing this.

Some think that the stock sway bars can be retained while others feel that sway bars should be upgraded to 1⅛ inch front and ⅞ inch rear. However, it is essential that all four springs be changed to lower the car to improve handling. Naturally, wide tires are necessary, and the newer Mustangs can accommodate rather large wheels (15x7 or 15x8) with no problem.

It is obvious that following all these recommendations will be expensive. Regardless of your budget, the first modification should be to upgrade the rear sway bar. A ¾ inch rear bar is recommended for the four- and six-cylinder cars; the 302 should have a ⅞ inch bar.

If your tires are ready for replacement, try to get the best tires you can afford. If you are planning to replace both wheels and tires, go for a 15x7 or 15x8 combination. Although the TRX system is good, you will have more flexibility if you go to conventional wheels and tires with greater size choice.

The same applies for the stock struts and shocks. If yours are ready for replacement, a good choice would be to use the Koni units available. It also helps if you replace the rear suspension rubber bushings with polyurethane bushings to reduce the rear suspension's compliance and limit wheel hop. The typical enthusiast won't mind the firmer ride.

Like the Mustang II, these newer Mustangs need additional horsepower to take full advantage of any suspension modifications you make. Ford is slowly improving the output of the 302, but an aftermarket intake manifold and a free-flowing exhaust system are necessary. It is not advisable to go beyond these simple modifications on the new Mustangs, because the rest of the driveline, such as the transmission and rear axle, aren't designed to handle a lot of power and torque. The rear axle is simply not strong enough, but there are conversions available to replace the stock rear with a nine-inch rear. Again, this will push up costs.

However, Ford knows the Mustang's problems and every year some improvement has been made. The quadra-shock rear (first available on the 1984 SVO Mustang) became standard on all 1985 GT's and has greatly transformed and cured many of the rear-end ills. The wider 15x7 inch wheels along with the Goodyear Gatorback Eagle tires are by far superior to the Michelin TRX tires. The 1985 Mustang GT, in terms of acceleration, is as fast as the 1965-66 Shelby GT350 and the 1969-70 Boss 302. Largely due to the wider wheels and tires it has become a much better handling car, although it can still be improved upon.

It is obvious that the newer Mustang is a fairly good handling car to begin with; however, in order to transform the car into a reliable late-sixties-type performer, it needs extensive modifications.

In this respect, older Mustangs, 1964-73 vintage, are easier and less expensive to modify because they are already equipped with heavier-duty driveline and suspension components. They do lack the refinement and up-to-date comforts that newer Mustangs have.

The choice is up to you.

The Kamei X-1 Mustang has received all the necessary suspension modifications. Wheels are Jongbloed modular units with B. F. Goodrich Comp/TA tires. Photo courtesy Kamei USA Auto Extras.

APPENDIX 1

UPPER CONTROL ARM RELOCATION INSTRUCTIONS
1964½-70 Mustangs

PARTS AND TOOLS REQUIRED
1. Template (photocopy from this book)
2. Jack, jackstands, lug wrench
3. ½ inch socket for shock absorbers
4. Spring compressor
5. ¾ inch wrench for control-arm mounting nuts
6. ½ inch drill with a 17/32 bit plus smaller bits for starting holes

INSTRUCTIONS
1. Jack car, remove front wheel and shock absorber.
2. Compress spring enough to be out of the way or remove it completely.
3. Support lower control arm and brake assembly on a jackstand.
4. Unbolt the control arm bolts from inside the engine compartment. Save the aligning shims (1964-66 *only*) and remember their original location.
5. Swing the upper control arm, rotor and spindle to the side. Be careful not to strain the brake line hose.
6. Use a photocopy of template provided. Trim out upper holes and bolt it in existing holes.
7. With template in place, mark centers for new holes using center punch.
8. Drill new holes starting with a small bit (¼ inch) and working your way to 17/32 inch.
9. Install upper control arm in new holes. For 1964-66, be sure to use the alignment shims in the same positions they came from. Remove an even thickness, about ⅛ inch to ¼ inch, of shims from each position to compensate for the increased positive camber.
10. Reassemble suspension.
11. Align front suspension to the following specifications:

<u>1964½-70 Mustang</u>

Caster	2 degrees positive
Camber	0 to ½ degree negative
Toe-in	⅛ inch

12. These templates are courtesy of the Shelby American Automobile Club.

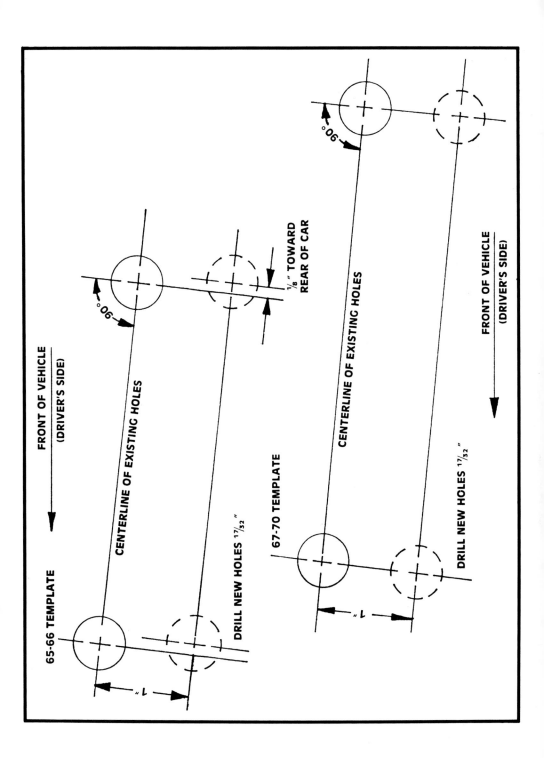

MUSTANG ENGINES

	TYPE	CUBIC INCHES	BORE X STROKE	HP@RPM	TORQUE (lbs.-ft) & RPM	CR	CARB	ENGINE CODE
1964½	I-6	170	3.50 x2.94	101@4400	156@2400	8.7	1V	U
	V-8	260	3.80 x2.87	164@4400	258@2200	8.8	2V	F
	V-8	289	4.00 x2.87	210@4400	300@2800	9.0	4V	A
1965	I-6	200	3.68 x3.13	120@4400	190@2400	9.2	1V	T
	V-8	289	4.00 x2.87	200@4400	282@2400	9.3	2V	C
	V-8	289	4.00 x2.87	225@4800	305@3200	10.0	4V	A
	V-8	289	4.00 x2.87	271@6000	312@3400	10.5	4V	K
	V-8	289 (Shelby)	4.00 x2.87	306@6000	329@4200	10.5	4V	K
1966	I-6	200	3.68 x3.13	120@4400	190@2400	9.2	1V	T
	V-8	289	4.00 x2.87	200@4400	282@2400	9.3	2V	C
	V-8	289	4.00 x2.87	225@4800	305@3200	10.0	4V	A
	V-8	289	4.00 x2.87	271@6000	312@3400	10.5	4V	K
	V-8	289 (Shelby)	4.00 x2.87	306@6000	329@4200	10.5	4V	K
1967	I-6	200	3.68 x3.13	120@4400	190@2400	9.2	1V	T
	V-8	289	4.00 x2.87	200@4400	282@2400	9.3	2V	C
	V-8	289	4.00 x2.87	225@4800	305@3200	10.0	4V	A
	V-8	289	4.00 x2.87	271@6000	312@3400	10.5	4V	K
	V-8	289 (Shelby)	4.00 x2.87	306@6000	329@4200	10.5	4V	K
	V-8	390	4.05 x3.78	320@4800	427@3200	10.5	4V	S
	V-8	427 (Shelby)	4.23 x3.78	425@6000	480@3700	11.0	8V	Q or S
	V-8	428 (Shelby)	4.13 x3.98	355@5400	420@3200	10.5	8V	Q or S
1968	I-6	200	3.68 x3.13	115@4400	190@2400	8.8	1V	T
	V-8	289	4.00 x2.87	195@4600	288@2600	8.7	2V	C
	V-8	302	4.00 x3.00	230@4800	310@2800	10.0	4V	J
	V-8	302 (Shelby)	4.00 x3.00	250@4800	310@2800	10.0	4V	J
	V-8	390	4.05 x3.78	265@4400	390@2600	9.5	2V	Y
	V-8	390	4.05 x3.78	325@4800	427@3200	10.5	4V	S
	V-8	427	4.23 x3.78	390@4600	460@3200	10.9	4V	W
	V-8	428CJ	4.13 x3.98	335@5600	440@3400	10.6	4V	R
	V-8	428 (Shelby)	4.13 x3.98	360@5400	420@3200	10.5	4V	S
1969	I-6	200	3.68 x3.13	115@2800	190@2200	8.8	1V	T
	I-6	250	3.68 x3.91	155@4000	240@1600	9.0	1V	L
	V-8	302	4.00 x3.00	220@4600	300@2600	9.5	2V	F
	V-8	302 Boss	4.00 x3.00	290@5800	290@4300	10.5	4V	G
	V-8	351W	4.00 x3.50	250@4600	355@2600	9.5	2V	H
	V-8	351W	4.00 x3.50	290@4800	385@3200	10.7	4V	M
	V-8	390	4.05 x3.78	320@4600	427@3200	10.5	4V	S
	V-8	428CJ, CJ-R	4.13 x3.98	335@5600	440@3400	10.6	4V	Q-CJ, R-CJ-R
	V-8	429 Boss	4.36 x3.59	375@5200	450@3400	10.5	4V	Z
1970	I-6	200	3.68 x3.13	120@4400	190@2900	8.0	1V	T
	I-6	250	3.68 x3.91	155@4000	240@1600	9.0	1V	L
	V-8	302	4.00 x3.00	220@4600	300@2600	9.5	2V	F
	V-8	302 Boss	4.00 x3.00	290@5800	290@4300	10.5	4V	G
	V-8	351W	4.00 x3.50	250@4600	355@2600	9.5	2V	H
	V-8	351C	4.00 x3.50	250@4600	355@2600	9.5	2V	H
	V-8	351C	4.00 x3.50	300@5400	380@3400	11.0	4V	M
	V-8	428CJ,CR-R	4.13 x3.98	335@5600	440@3400	10.6	4V	Q-CJ, R-CJ-R
	V-8	429 Boss	4.36 x3.59	375@5200	450@3400	10.5	4V	Z
1971	I-6	250	3.68 x3.91	145@4000	232@1600	9.0	1V	L
	V-8	302	4.00 x3.00	210@4600	296@2600	9.0	2V	F
	V-8	351C	4.00 x3.50	240@4600	350@2600	9.0	2V	H
	V-8	351C-CJ	4.00 x3.50	280@5400	370@3400	9.0	4V	M
	V-8	351C	4.00 x3.50	285@5400	370@3400	10.7	4V	M
	V-8	351C Boss	4.00 x3.50	330@5400	370@4000	11.7	4V	R
	V-8	429CJ-R	4.36 x3.59	370@5400	450@3400	11.3	4V	C
	V-8	429SCJ-R	4.36 x3.59	375@5600	450@3400	11.3	4V	J, C, non ram air
1972	I-6	250	3.68 x3.91	98@3400	197@1600	8.0	1V	L
	V-8	302	4.00 x3.00	140@4000	239@2000	8.5	2V	F
	V-8	351C	4.00 x3.50	177@4000	284@2000	8.6	2V	H
	V-8	351C-CJ	4.00 x3.50	266@5400	301@3600	9.0	4V	Q
	V-8	351C-HO	4.00 x3.50	275@6000	286@3800	9.2	4V	R

	TYPE	CUBIC INCHES	BORE X STROKE	HP@RPM	TORQUE (lbs.-ft) & RPM	CR	CARB	ENGINE CODE
1973	I-6	250	3.68 x3.91	99@3600	184@1600	8.0	1V	L
	V-8	302	4.00 x3.00	141@4000	242@2000	8.0	2V	F
	V-8	351C	4.00 x3.50	177@4000	284@2000	8.6	2V	H
	V-8	351C-CJ	4.00 x3.50	266@5400	301@3600	9.0	4V	Q
1974	I-4	140	3.781x3.126	88@5000	116@2600	8.4	2V	Y
	V-6	170.8	3.66 x2.70	105@4600	140@3200	8.2	2V	Z
1975	I-4	140	3.781x3.126	88@5000	116@2600	9.0	2V	Y
	V-6	170.8	3.66 x2.70	105@4600	140@3200	8.7	2V	Z
	V-8	302	4.00 x3.00	140@4200	234@2200	8.0	2V	F
1976	I-4	140	3.781x3.126	88@5000	116@2600	9.0	2V	Y
	V-6	170.8	3.66 x2.70	105@4600	140@3200	8.7	2V	Z
	V-8	302	4.00 x3.00	140@4200	234@2200	8.0	2V	F
1977	I-4	140	3.781x3.126	92@5000	121@3000	9.0	2V	Y
	V-6	170.8	3.66 x2.70	103@4300	149@2800	8.7	2V	Z
	V-8	302	4.00 x3.00	134@3600	247@1800	8.4	2V	F
1978	I-4	140	3.781x3.126	88@4800	118@2800	9.0	2V	Y
	V-6	170.8	3.66 x2.70	90@4200	143@2200	8.7	2V	Z
	V-8	302	4.00 x3.00	139@3600	250@1600	8.4	2V	F
1979	I-4	140	3.781x3.126	88@4800	118@2800	9.0	2V	Y
	I-4	140 Turbo	3.781x3.126	132@5500	142@3500	9.0	2V	W
	V-6	170.8	3.66 x2.70	109@4800	142@2800	8.7	2V	Z
	I-6	200	3.68 x3.13	85@3600	154@1600	8.5	1V	T
	V-8	302	4.00 x3.00	140@3600	250@1800	8.5	2V	F
1980	I-4 MT	140	3.781x3.126	88@4800	118@2800	9.0	2V	A
	I-4 AT	140	3.781x3.126	90@4800	125@2600	9.0	2V	A
	I-4 Turbo	140	3.781x3.126	135@6000	143@2800	9.0	2V	T
	I-6	200 MT	3.68 x3.13	91@3800	160@1600	8.6	1V	B
	I-6	200 AT	3.68 x3.13	94@4000	157@2000	8.6	1V	B
	V-8	255	3.68 x3.00	119@3800	194@2200	8.8	2V	D
1981	I-4	140	3.781x3.126	88@4600	118@2600	9.0	2V	A
	I-6	200	3.68 x3.13	94@4000	158@1400	8.6	1V	B
	V-8	255	3.68 x3.00	120@3400	205@2200	8.2	2V	D
1982	I-4	140	3.781x3.126	88@4600	118@2600	9.0	2V	A
	I-6	200	3.68 x3.13	94@4000	158@1400	8.6	1V	B
	V-8	255	3.68 x3.00	120@3400	205@2200	8.2	2V	D
	V-8	302	4.00 x3.00	157@4200	240@2400	8.4	2V	F
1983	I-4	140	3.781x3.126	88@4600	118@2600	9.0	1V	A
	V-6	232	3.814x3.388	112@4000	175@2600	8.6	2V	3
	V-8	302 HO	4.00 x3.00	175@4000	245@2400	8.3	4V	F
1984	I-4	140	3.781x3.126	88@4000	122@2400	9.0	1V	A
	I-4 Turbo GT	140	3.781x3.126	145@4600	180@3600	8.0	EFI	T
	I-4 SVO	140	3.781x3.126	175@4400	210@3000	8.0	EFI	T
	V-6	232	3.68 x3.00	120@3600	205@1600	8.6	EFI	3
	V-8	302 HO	4.00 x3.00	175@4000	245@2200	8.3	4V	F
	V-8	302 HO	4.00 x3.00	205@4400	265@3200	8.3	4V-dual exhaust	F
	V-8	302 HO	4.00 x3.00	165@4000	245@2000	8.3	EFI	F
1985	I-4	140	3.781x3.126	88@4400	122@2600	9.5	1V	A
	I-4 SVO	140	3.781x3.126	205@5000	248@3000	8.0	EFI	T
	V-6	232	3.68 x3.00	120@3600	205@1600	8.7	EFI	3
	V-8	302 HO	4.00 x3.00	165@3800	245@2000	8.4	EFI	F
	V-8	302 HO	4.00 x3.00	210@4600	265@3400	8.4	4V-dual exhaust	F

APPENDIX 3

REAR AXLE CODES – 1964–1985

Axle	1965	1966	1967	1968	1969	1970	1971	1972	1973	1974	1975-76	1977-78	1979	1980	1981	1982	1983	1984	1985
2.35					F														
2.47													B	B(C)	B(C)	B(C)			
2.50				0															
2.73														8	8(M)	8(M)	8(M)	8(M)	8(M)
2.75			8(H)	1(A)	2(K)	2(K)	2(K)	2(K)	2(K)										
2.79				2(B)	3	3	3	3	3		3	3							
2.80	6(F)	6(F)	6(F)	3(C)	4(M)	4(M)	4(M)												
2.83	2(B)	2(B)	2(B)	4(D)	5	5													
3.00	1(A)	1(A)	1(A)	5(E)	6(O)	6	6	6	6(O)		6(O)								
3.07						B	B												
3.08					C(U)	C							Y(Z)	Y(Z)	Y(Z)	Y(Z)	Y(Z)	Y(Z)	Y(Z)
3.10					7														
3.18												4							
3.20	3(C)	3(C)	3(C)	6(F)															
3.25	4(D)	4(D)	4(D)	7(G)	9(R)	9(R)	9(R)	9(R)											
3.27											7								
3.40																			
3.45													F(R)	F(R)	F(R)	F(R)	F(R)	F(R)	F(R)
3.50	5(E)	5(E)	5(E)	8(H)	A(S)	A(S)	9(R)	A(S)	9(R)								5(E)	5(E)	5(E)
3.55										G(X)	G(X)								
3.73																			(W)
3.89	8(H)	8(H)					A(S)		A(S)										
3.91	9(I)	9(I)	9(I)																
4.11					(V)	(V)	(V)	(V)											
4.30					(W)	(W)	(Y)												

Letter in parentheses indicates locking differential.

APPENDIX 4

MUSTANG TRANSMISSIONS 1964½-73

	CODE
Three-speed manual	1
Four-speed manual, wide ratio	5
Four-speed manual, close ratio	6 (1967-71)
Four-speed manual, close ratio	E (1972-73)
Three-speed automatic C4	W
Three-speed automatic FMX	X
Three-speed automatic C6	U

MUSTANG TRANSMISSIONS 1974-85

	CODE
Four-speed overdrive (SROD)	4
Five-speed manual	5
Five-speed manual overdrive (RAP)	5
Four-speed manual (Borg-Warner)	6
Four-speed overdrive (RUG)	7
Four-speed (ET)	7
Three-speed automatic C3	V
Three-speed automatic C4	W
Three-speed automatic C5	C
AOD (automatic overdrive)	T

APPENDIX 5

MUSTANG SPECIFICATIONS

	1964-66	1967-68	1969-70	1971-73	1974-78	1979-85
Wheelbase, in.	108	108	108	109	96.2	100.4
Track, frt./rear, in.	56/56	58.1/58/1	58.5/58.5	61.5/61.5	55.6/55.8	56.6/57
Width, in.	68.2	70.9	71.8	74.1	70.2	69.1
Height, in.	51	51.8	50.3	50.1	50.3	51.9
Length, in.	181.6	183.6	187.4	189.5[1]	175	179.1
Curb weight, lb.	2,860 (289)	2,980 (302)	3,625 (428CJ)	3,560 (351CJ)	3,290 (302)	2,861 (140)[2]
Wt. dist., % f/r	53/47 (289)	56/44 (302)	59/41 (428CJ)	56.5/43.5 (351)	59/41	57/43[3]

1–193.8 in 1973
2–3075 with 302
3–59/41 with 302

APPENDIX 6

CLUBS AND DIRECTORIES

SHELBY AMERICAN AUTOMOBILE CLUB
22 Olmstead Road
West Redding, CT 06896
203-438-7470
Club dedicated to Shelby Mustangs, Cobras, Ford GT's and Tigers. Many regional groups. Publishes *The Shelby American* five times per year.

MUSTANG OWNER'S CLUB INTERNATIONAL
2829 Cagua Dr. N.E.
Albuquerque, NM 87110
505-881-2715
For all Mustang owners and enthusiasts. Publishes *The Pony Express,* a monthly newsletter.

MUSTANG CLUB OF AMERICA
P.O. Box 447
Lithonia, GA 30058
404-482-4822
For 1964½-85 Mustangs and Shelbys.
Many regional groups. Publishes the
Mustang Times, a monthly magazine.

PERFORMANCE FORD CLUB OF
AMERICA
P.O. Box 32
Ashville, OH 43103
Publishes *The Ford Enthusiast* six
times per year. Covers the world of
Ford performance.

BOSS 429 MUSTANG DIRECTORY
S. 4228 Conklin
Spokane, WA 99203
Dedicated to registering and collecting information on Boss 429 Mustangs. Publishes occasional progress
reports.

BOSS 302 REGISTRY
Randy Ream
1817 Janet Ave.
Lebanon, PA 17042
Dedicated to registering and collect-
ing information on Boss 302 Mustangs.
Publishes occasional progress re-
ports.

'71 429 MUSTANG REGISTRY
P.O. Box 1472
Fair Oaks, CA 95628
Dedicated to tracing down the last
big-block Mustangs.

BOSS 351 DIRECTORY
Harry McLean, Jr.
Rt. 5 Box 475
Spokane, WA 99208
Dedicated to collecting and register-
ing information on Boss 351 Mustangs.

APPENDIX 7

SUGGESTED READING

PERIODICALS:
TOTAL PERFORMANCE MAGAZINE
28562 Coleridge Ave.
Hayward, CA 94544
An excellent source of up-to-the-minute Ford racing coverage, as well as
Ford performance features and information.
MUSTANG MONTHLY
P.O. Box 5817
Lakeland, FL 33803
Covers 1964½-73 Mustangs. Although written primarily for the Mustang
restorer and collector it is of value to performance-oriented enthusiasts.
HOT ROD'S MUSTANG
Petersen Publishing Company
8490 Sunset Blvd.
Los Angeles, CA 90069
Published quarterly. Many interesting articles on Mustang modification and
performance.
FABULOUS MUSTANGS
Argus Publishers Corporation
12301 Wilshire Blvd.
Los Angeles, CA 90069
Published quarterly. Similar to *Hot Rod's Mustang;* covers new and old
Mustangs.

BOOKS:

The following are all published by HP Books, P.O. Box 5367, Tucson, AZ 85703

How to rebuild your small-block Ford, by Tom Monroe. 160 pp., sftbnd. Covers all 221, 225, 260, 289, HP289, 302 Boss 302, 351W engines.

How to rebuild your Ford V-8, 351C-351M-400-429-460, by Tom Monroe. 160 pp., sftbnd.

How to rebuild your big-block Ford, by Steve Christ. 160 pp., sftbnd. Covers all FE Series big-blocks including 390, 427, 428, 428CJ/SCJ.

Holley Carburetors & Manifolds, by Mike Urich & Bill Fisher. 160 pp., sftbnd. An excellent book.

How To Make Your Car Handle, by Fred Puhn. 200 pp., sftbnd. An excellent guide to the world of handling and suspension design.

The following are published by Petersen Specialty Publications, 8490 Sunset Blvd., Los Angeles, CA 90069. Each is an informative manual on its subject.

Basic Auto Repair Manual

Basic Cams, Valves and Exhaust Systems

Basic Carburetion and Fuel Systems

Basic Chassis, Suspension and Brakes

Basic Clutches and Transmissions

Basic Ignition and Electrical Systems

The following are published by S-A Design Publishing, 515 W. Lambert, Bldg. E. Brea, CA 92621.

Ford Performance: Includes All Modern Ford Performance Engines, by Pat Ganahl. 125 pp., sftbnd. An excellent guide to modifying Ford V-8 engines.

The Complete Guide to Bolt-On Performance. 160 pp., sftbnd. An interesting and informative guide.

V-6 Performance, by Pat Ganahl. 128 pp., sftbnd. Although it covers mostly GM V-6 engines, it has chapters on Ford 2600-2800 and 3.8 V-6 engines.

Peformance With Economy, by David Vizard. 128 pp., sftbnd. Easy-to-read guide on how to get performance with economy.

Smokey Yunick's Power Secrets, by Smokey Yunick and Larry Schreib. 128 pages, sftbnd. Although it covers Chevy engines, much of Smokey's experience is helpful to Ford owners.

Holley Carburetors, by Dave Emanuel. 128 pp., sftbnd. Excellent guide for the modification of Holley carburetors.

The following are reprints of factory Ford information available during the late sixties to early seventies available from Classic Motorbooks, Osceola, WI.

Ford Off Highway Parts & Modifications Manual, 108 pp.

Boss 302 Chassis Modification, 30 pp.

Boss 302 Engine Modification, 26 pp.

Illustrated High Performance Mustang Buyer's Guide, by Peter C. Sessler. 150 pp., sftbnd. An excellent reference/guide covering 1965-73 performance Mustangs.

New Directions in Suspension Design: Making the Fast Car Faster, by Colin Cambell. 213 pp., hdbnd. An interesting and readable book for those wanting to learn more about handling.

Advanced Race Car Suspension Development, by Steve Smith. 168 pp. Emphasis is on stock-car setup but it is interesting reading and useful for other racing applications.

PARTS SOURCES

The following companies and individuals are just a few that cater to the needs of the Mustang enthusiast.

ACCEL
P.O. Box 142
Branford, CT 06405
Ignition components

ADDCO INDUSTRIES INC.
Watertower Road
Lake Park, FL 33403
305-844-2531
Antisway bars

AMERICAN EXHAUST INDUSTRIES
18933 S. Reyes
Compton, CA 90221
Manufacturers of Blackjack and Cyclone headers and exhaust system components

AR INCORPORATED
P.O. Box 6358
Ventura, CA 93006
Boss 429 engine components

AUTOCRAFT MOTORING ACCESSORIES
2210 W. Lincoln
Anaheim, CA 92801
213-924-8334
1979-up Mustang parts

AUTOTRONIC CONTROLS CORPORATION
6908 Commerce
El Paso, TX 79915
Ignition components

B&A FORD PERFORMANCE INC.
Box 6553
Fort Smith, AR 72906
918-626-3997
351C heads to 289/302 conversion kits

B&M AUTOMOTIVE PRODUCTS
9152 Independence Avenue
Chatsworth, CA 91311
Automatic transmission components

CLASSIC MOTORBOOKS, INC.
729 Prospect Avenue
Osceola, WI 54020
715-294-3345
Automotive literature

CLIFFORD RESEARCH & DEVELOPMENT CO., INC.
15572 Computer Lane
Huntington Beach, CA 92649
Six-cylinder headers

COMPETITION CAMS INC.
2806 Hanger Road
Memphis, TN 38818
901-795-2400
Camshafts and valvetrain components

CRANE CAMS INC.
P.O. Box 160
Hallandale, FL 33009
Camshafts and valvetrain components

CURRIE ENTERPRISES
206 S. Highland
Placentia, CA 92670
714-528-6957
Ford rear end specialist

DAN WILLIAMS
1210 N.E. 130 Street
North Miami, FL 33161
305-893-5123
Four-speed transmission specialist (Top Loader)

DOBI
320 Thor Place
Brea, CA 92621
714-529-1977
1979-up Mustang/Capri parts and accessories

EARL'S SUPPLY COMPANY
825 E. Sepuvelda
Carson, CA 90745
213-830-1620
Stainless steel hosing

EASTERN MUSTANG SPECIALTY
646 South Road
Poughkeepsie, NY 12601
914-462-6006
New, used Mustang parts

ED ISKENDERIAN CAMS
16020 S. Broadway
Gardena, CA 90247
Camshafts and valvetrain components

EDELBROCK CORPORATION
411 Coral Circle
El Segundo, CA 90245
Intake manifolds

ESSLINGER ENGINEERING
712 Montecito Drive
San Gabriel, CA 91776
818-289-3073
2300 engine components

FAIR PERFORMANCE FORD
P.O. Box 192
Mt. Dora, FL 32757
904-383-0655
New and used Ford engine parts

THE FORD EMPORIUM
555 Hillside Drive
Coldwater, MI 49036
New and used Ford parts

FORD MOTORSPORT
PERFORMANCE EQUIPMENT
Ford Motor Company
17000 Southfield Road
Allen Park, MI 48101
Factory Ford engine components
and accessories

FORD POWER PARTS
14504 S. Carmenita No. C
Norwalk, CA 90650
213-921-5300
New and used Ford engine parts

GLAZIER'S MUSTANG BARN
531 Wambold Road
Souderton, PA 18964
800-523-6708
New and used Mustang parts

HEDMAN HEADERS
9599 West Jefferson
Culver City, CA 90230
Headers and exhaust systems

HOLLEY REPLACEMENT PARTS
DIV.
11955 East Nine Mile Road
Warren, MI 48090
Carburetors

HOOKER HEADERS
1032 W. Brooks Street
Ontario, CA 91761
714-983-5871
Headers and exhaust systems

IECO
1431-A Broadway
Santa Monica, CA 90404
Mustang II parts

INGLESE INDUCTION SYSTEMS
INC.
11 Tipping Drive
Branford, CT 06403
203-481-5544
Exotic induction systems

JIM WICKS
P.O. Box 84
Fairland, OK 74343
918-256-7121
New and used Ford parts

JR HEADERS
470 Knowes Road
N. Adams, MI 49262
Exhaust headers

KAMEI USA AUTO EXTRAS
300 Montonese Avenue
North Haven, CT 06473
1974-up Mustang spoilers

K&N ENGINEERING INC.
P.O. 1329
Riverside, CA 92502
High-performance air filters

KAUFMANN PRODUCTS
Advanced Engineering West
12418½ Benedict Avenue
Downey, CA 90242
213-803-3677
1979-up Mustang/Capri engine parts
and accessories

KONI AMERICA INC.
P.O. Box 40
Culpeper, VA 22701
Shock absorbers

MAIER RACING ENTERPRISES
235 Laurel Avenue
Hayward, CA 94541
415-581-7600
1964½-85 Mustang parts and
accessories

MALLORY IGNITION
1801 Oregon Street
Carson City, NV 89701
702-882-6600
Ignition components

MAREMONT CORPORATION
Gabriel Shocks and Struts Div.
200 E. Randolph Drive
Chicago, IL 60601
Shock absorbers and struts

MIDWEST SPECIALTY AUTOS
25981 Lake Drive
Coldwater, MI 49036
517-238-2262
New and used Ford parts

MILODON ENGINEERING
9152 Independence Avenue
Chatsworth, CA 91311
Deep sump oil pans

MOROSO PERFORMANCE
PRODUCTS INC.
Carter Drive
Guilford, CT 06437
203-453-6571
Oil pans, engine and driveline
components

MUSTANGS UNLIMITED
63 Tolland Turnpike
Manchester, CT 06040
800-243-7278
New and used Mustang parts

OFFENHAUSER SALES
CORPORATION
5232 Alhambra Avenue
Los Angeles, CA 90032
213-225-1307
Intake manifolds

PAXTON SUPERCHARGERS
929 Olympic Boulevard
Santa Monica, CA 90404
213-394-2751
Superchargers

PERFORMANCE AUTOMOTIVE
WHOLESALE
19441 Business Center Drive
Northridge, CA 91324
Ford engine kits

PERFORMANCE MOETORS LTD.
3310 South Minnesota
Sioux Falls, SD 57105
605-335-3183
Ford engines and parts

THE PERFORMANCE PEOPLE
Mr. Gasket, Hayes, Lakewood
4566 Spring Road
Cleveland, Ohio 44131
216-398-8300
Accessories, clutch and driveline
parts

PRO STOCK ENGINEERING
16102 Orange Avenue
Paramount, CA 90723
213-630-4080
Ford engine parts

QUICKOR ENGINEERING
6710 S.W. 111th
Beaverton, OR 97005
503-646-9696
Mustang suspension parts

RACER WALSH CO.
Bel-Ans Park
Orangeburg, NY 10962
914-365-0500
2300 engine parts, suspension
components, accessories

RANCHO SUSPENSION
6309 Paramount Boulevard
P.O. Box 5429
Long Beach, CA 90805
1979-up Mustang suspension kits

RHOADS LIFTERS
326 1000 East North
Taylor, AZ 85939
605-536-7503
Variable rate hydraulic lifters

RUSSELL PERFORMANCE
PRODUCTS INC.
20420 S. Susana Road
Carson, CA 90745
Stainless steel hosing

SHELBY INTERNATIONAL
4558 Brazil
Los Angeles, CA 90039
Wheels

STAM-BAR STABILIZERS
2609 Janna Avenue
Modesto, CA 95350
209-523-7607
1964-73 Mustang antisway bars

STAINLESS STEEL BRAKES CORP.
11470 Main Road
Clarence, NY 14031
800-448-7722
Stainless steel brakes

STEVE STRANGE
Boss Performance
P.O. Box 8035
Spokane, WA 99203
Boss 429 parts

THRUSH INCORPORATED
172 Bethridge Road
Rexdale, Ontario, Canada M9W 1N3
416-746-4422
High-performance mufflers

TONY D. BRANDA SHELBY &
MUSTANG PARTS
1434 E. Pleasant Valley Boulevard
Altoona, PA 16602
800-458-3477
Mustang and Shelby parts

TOTAL PERFORMANCE INC.
40631 Irwin
Mt. Clemens, MI 48045
313-468-FORD
New, used Ford engines and parts,
driveline specialists

TURBO CITY
1123 W. Collins
Orange, CA 92667
714-639-4993
Turbochargers

VINDICATOR RACING
ENTERPRISES
47 Pleasantville Road
Pleasantville, NY 10570
914-769-1800
New, used Ford engine parts

WEIAND AUTOMOTIVE
P.O. Box 65977
Los Angeles, CA 90065
Intake manifolds